MIDLAND RED STYLE

Roger Torode and Malcolm Keeley

with the assistance
of the collections of
Michael Rooum
The Transport Museum, Wythall
The Kithead Trust
Ken Jubb

Capital Transport

Acknowledgements

The authors thank all those who have contributed to this book through the loan of material from their collections. The publicity material comes primarily from the collections of Roger Torode and Mike Rooum. Mike generously gave access to his splendid collection gathered over many years, as did Malcolm Keeley, Mike Greenwood, David Hale, Patrick Kingston, Peter Newland, the Kithead Trust and the Omnibus Society Library. Many of the 1950s posters come from the collection of the Transport Museum, Wythall and we thank those who kindly donated them to the museum for us all to enjoy. Roger also thanks Mike Walton at the London Transport Museum for his encouragement in developing the book.

The quite exceptional help of Ken Jubb in providing photographs must be recorded, together with the sourcing assistance of Mike Jordan from Wythall and Michael Eyre, the latter also kindly enhancing many images. Sincere thanks are also due to Paul Gray and Peter Jaques for kindly checking the manuscript, although the authors rightly take the blame for any surviving errors. Notable source books for information have been the fleet histories of the company produced jointly several decades ago by the PSV Circle and Omnibus Society, and the two volumes by Messrs Gray, Keeley and Seale, published by the Transport Publishing Company in 1978-9. The excellent book 'Stratford Blue' by Robert L Telfer, published by Tempus Publishing, provided some information on Midland Red's fondly remembered subsidiary.

First published 2011

ISBN 978-185414-347-1

Published by Capital Transport Publishing
www.capitaltransport.com

Printed by 1010 Printing International Ltd

© Roger Torode and Malcolm Keeley 2011

Above Window posters proclaim 'Another new Midland Red bus to be placed at your service' as Brush-bodied S6 3070 indulges in a spot of company publicity around Birmingham, here passing the Hall of Memory. It entered service at Banbury in May 1947. These S6s must have looked so modern – at this time, Birmingham City Transport had not received any post-war vehicles. *Courtesy of Kithead Trust*

Title page Midland Red's most famous operation was the Motorway Express service, started on the day the M1 opened, 2 November 1959. The CM5T coaches were specially developed for it and cruised to London at 80 mph. 4801 is seen with a sister vehicle at Victoria Coach Station. *Tony Wilson*

Rear cover This is Midland Red as most like to remember it. Bright red double-deckers loading up in a busy, sunlit bus station, in this case Worcester with BMMO D9 5379 prominent in 1969. *Ken Jubb*

HEREFORD

The passage of time has dealt kindly with Hereford, its ancient and historic beauty delighting the eye of many a visitor

Contents

Introduction

'The bus operating company which has so often pointed the way for the makers' designers to follow' – an ecstatic response by a 'Motor Transport' reporter reviewing the latest BMMO product.

Midland Red was the largest bus operator in the UK outside London. It operated over 1,900 buses and coaches at its peak, covering 12,000 square miles with a route mileage of around 6,500. In 1956, 79 million miles were operated and 484 million passengers carried. A total of 1,150 separate stage carriage services ran through 15 counties while a large and immaculate fleet of coaches were known throughout the country, offering top quality cruises and long-distance express services.

To operate this empire required over thirty garages, plus offices, enquiry bureaux and other support premises. Most notable among the latter was Carlyle Works. Here another extraordinary feature of this bus company becomes significant. In addition to the usual business of maintaining, repairing and overhauling, for around fifty years Midland Red actually designed and built its own buses. For many years this was just the chassis and engines with coach-builders producing most of the bodies to the company's exacting designs. After the rebuild of 'Carlyle', relaunched as Central Works in 1954, the complete vehicles were built there. These were practical, advanced and often stylish buses and coaches – they were always individualistic. Midland Red frequently led the industry, hence the outburst by the reporter at the beginning of this piece.

Midland Red built up rapidly from the early years of the twentieth century. It developed travel by bus and coach for work, leisure and tourism throughout the Midlands, and connecting the Midlands by road to the rest of the country. In doing so, it produced some of the finest publicity by a British bus and coach operator.

Malcolm Keeley has written books for over thirty years on the various aspects of Midland Red. Roger Torode also grew up in Midland Red territory and was similarly impressed by the quality of its operations, vehicles, posters and publicity. He used its buses, travelled to holidays in its coaches and, like Malcolm, took trips with its Day Anywhere tickets.

Roger moved to London when 20 and, throughout his career with London Transport, was well aware of the high regard in which its transport publicity (and that of the railway industry) was justifiably held, with books, exhibitions, and auctions. Midland Red's very attractive publicity material, however, is not so well known.

While the Underground group and London Transport were able to commission leading artists and became patrons of poster art in Britain, Midland Red had to follow a less costly course, but the company nevertheless commissioned well-designed contemporary material. Under the inspired leadership of O C Power and his publicity chief, J P Savage, the company produced well-designed material to inform the public and to encourage them to use Midland Red's rapidly expanding services. In doing so, they promoted the Midlands, its towns, cities and countryside, together with the holiday destinations that Midland Red's services brought within reach.

Unfortunately, many of the publicity items shown in this book are not dated, nor are the artists known. The date has sometimes been determined from the vehicles shown or from information in the advertisements. However, it may have been left off deliberately, to avoid shortening the shelf life of the publication. The publicity material shown here has been copied and digitally restored by Roger.

In addition to the paper publicity, this book looks at Midland Red style in many forms – from buses to booking offices and coaches to concrete lintels, stop plates to posters and leaflets to letterheads.

Authors' favourite. The 1926 SOS FS char-a-bancs looked cute but drivers found being separated from their tour passengers inconvenient.
E V Trigg collection

Top An advertising board showing the CI coach of 1948. Midland Red were once again several years ahead of other manufacturers.
Below 1935 SOS OLR touring coach.

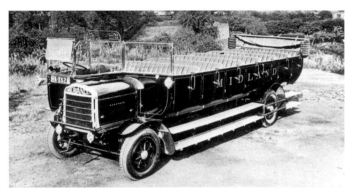

Midland Red Art – A Summary

Midland Red developed rapidly in the 1920s and '30s and needed to promote its expanding network of services. James Savage had worked before the First World War at BET headquarters in London and would have been well aware of the public transport publicity developed in London and by the railway companies.

The material he developed reflected the spirit of the times. The "roaring twenties" brought many changes to peoples' lives. Better communication and more leisure activities improved their standard of living. There was greater mobility in housing and employment, and women enjoyed more freedom and employment opportunities. The rapid expansion of mass travel by train and bus brought much greater personal freedom to almost everybody.

Midland Red brought these developments to the people of the Midlands. An article in an Edgbaston magazine in 1921 enthusiastically reported that *"Few services have contributed more effectively or extensively to promote the happiness and well-being of the people than that of the now familiar Midland "Red" motor omnibuses. These are the last word in mechanical road conveyance and traverse routes which radiate in all directions from Birmingham, and even link up the Midlands with the sea.*

Of comparatively recent development, they have revived the spirit of the old coaching days, without any of the disadvantages which were incidental to long journeys. Speed, cleanliness, comfort and safety – with opportunities of seeing country districts and villages remote from railway lines – these are the recommendations of the "Red" motor 'bus."

Midland Red's publicity and vehicles developed to reflect the Art Deco style of the '20s and '30s. Travel and transport was one of Art Deco's themes, and while it often focused on luxury trains, cars and the 'silversides' coaches of the USA, it also stressed elegance and comfort.

James Savage wrote an article on 'Selling Transport in the Midlands' for Bus and Coach Magazine in 1931. He stressed the need to look beyond morning and evening traffic for "tour and trip traffic", providing facilities for outings "if only to use surplus vehicles on days when ordinary traffic is slack". He saw this is an opportunity during the week, not just at weekends, and one that required persuasive advertising material in addition to the information that bus companies generally produced. This was a challenge, as the advertising had to be constantly fresh and creative. Routes and beauty spots were promoted according to the season of the year and considerable use was made of local newspapers and handbills. The company published regular folders of leaflets for each district with details of tours, long distance and seaside services. To constantly attract the public, posters and publicity were in vivid colours, booking and enquiry offices were designed to be bright by day and by night, and he found it fortunate that the company's colour was "red" as it made their premises easily recognisable. He had been told that, in passing Midland Red offices, "the public run the risk of permanent eye injury due to the vividness of the colours"!

Midland Red posters might be changed every week in the summer months to keep them topical, reflecting the season and current events. Savage recognised the magnificent posters of the railway companies, which were often works of art, and saw the importance of Midland Red posters in educating the public in getting out of the towns and into the countryside.

A raised relief map of the Midlands was displayed in larger windows, made of plaster with exaggerated contours and coloured to show towns, villages, rivers and Midland Red services. These would be illuminated at night and provided a continuous source

JAMES SAVAGE

James Percival Savage joined Midland Red in 1919, having previously been at BET Headquarters in London. In October 1901, at the age of 16, he was engaged as a clerk at the offices at Kingsway, and subsequently became Private Secretary to Emile Garcke and other BET Directors. In the First World War, he enlisted in the Artists' Rifles where he was commissioned as a Second Lieutenant and served in the Middle East. He was decorated with the Military Cross for conspicuous gallantry and devotion to duty and concluded his army service with the rank of Captain.

In May 1919 James Savage joined Midland Red as Personal Assistant to O C Power. The company was by then developing rapidly and a publicity department was created with him in charge. He also became responsible for advertising on buses and for the company's publications. He was Editor of the Midland Red Bulletin and Magazine from its beginning in 1932 until it ceased in 1939.

During the Second World War he became Corps Officer of the St John Ambulance Brigade, responsible for co-ordinating the Ambulance Divisions attached to many Midland Red garages. He was Honorary Treasurer of the National Passenger Transport Ambulance Association, which promoted First Aid competitions amongst teams from around the country. He retired from the position of Publicity and Advertising Superintendent at the end of April 1953.

It is interesting to note that, when he worked at BET Headquarters in London, Savage was a stone's throw from the Central School of Art which was set up by the London County Council in 1896, and where Edward Johnson ran a lively poster design course. It was this college that produced posters for the LCC tramways.

Johnson later worked for the Underground group, where he designed the London roundel and the Johnson font used for all London Transport publicity.

of interest to passers by. The company also supplied wall maps to schools, showing local geographical points together with bus routes.

Publicity books were all designed, illustrated and compiled by Midland Red's own publicity staff. Advertising and printing would be handled by a contractor, but the company wanted to retain control of the material and its publication. As a result, copy could be revised each year.

Aware of the continental practice of giving passengers an illustrated folder about points of interest on their journey, Savage developed a range of booklets. The Illustrated Guide to the ordinary bus services described the chief points of interest on the main services, following regular requests to conductors for information. The Holiday Tours and Seaside Service Book provided similar information for long distance services. The Private Party Book was given to anyone making an enquiry about arranging day trips who, Savage noted, often want to arrange a trip but 'have not the faintest idea where they want to go'! The Mascot Tour Book was designed to popularise the ordinary day and half-day tours. About 50 of the 120 tours were illustrated by a 'mascot' suggested by the outline of the route drawn on a map. Many of these attractive books had found their way into family homes for study by children and their parents – which is just what Midland Red wanted. Lastly, the Circular Tour Books were published to assist passengers planning trips with Day Anywhere tickets. They were also used by commercial travellers making their rounds by bus.

James Savage wrote that 'a good map is undoubtedly splendid propaganda for getting services well known and keeping the facilities in front of the public.' Midland Red's maps of the '20s and '30s reflect a feature of the best maps: they are works of art that are visually pleasing in order to convey information successfully. They were designed to appeal to potential travellers, including illustrations of the destinations that could be reached with brief notes of interest on the reverse, and they were distributed in large numbers.

Publicity material became simpler during World War Two, conveying basic information with the minimum of materials. As services resumed and expanded after the war and through the 1950s the style of enquiry offices, maps and timetables became more functional, reflecting the period and the less brash style of new General Manager Donald Sinclair. Nevertheless posters, guidebooks and leaflets continued to encourage travel, attracting people to the journey and their destinations. A particularly appealing range of posters was displayed on buses, garages and in enquiry offices proudly promoting the company, its services and its many achievements.

In addition to its own publicity, Midland Red's vehicles were in the forefront of vehicle design and technical developments. The company's suppliers were keen to show their involvement, and so manufacturers' advertisements in the technical press often promoted Midland Red vehicles. These provide further evidence of the importance of the Midland Red Style.

A fine publicity shot of FS HA3531, matching the pose of many of the line drawings. The bus was built in 1926 with a longer wheelbase and shorter cab than other FSs, and is thought to have been a prototype for the Q which followed in 1927. When new, it was used as a demonstrator to other operators interested in buying SOS buses. *The Transport Museum, Wythall, collection*

From before 1920 and up to the 1960s, Midland 'Red' publicity was illustrated by a series of highly accurate line drawings of buses and occasionally buildings, trucks and even horses. These were to a consistent style and are thought to have been produced by the 'bleach-out' process, in which the outlines of the photograph are sketched on the print, and the black metallic silver image is bleached away to leave a drawn outline. Passengers and crew could then be added by the artist. A copper printing plate would be produced from the drawing and would be used intensively on publicity material. The earliest drawing is of a TS bus on the 1917 timetable book, and most vehicle types are then covered up to the C2, LD8 and S13.

This work would need a skilled artist, and the similarity of the drawings suggests that they were by the same person. The artist is not identified, though they started at around the time that James Savage arrived at Midland Red, and they include vehicles introduced up to his retirement. Later vehicles were shown by photographs or drawn in a very different style, though the line drawings of earlier vehicles continued to be used for some years. James Savage would certainly have been responsible for commissioning the drawings, but as he had artists' skills, and as wherever possible work was done in-house, it seems likely that he drew them himself.

The technique would allow a drawing to be added to a scene created by another artist, as on the Helps to Happy Holidays title page *(page 46)*. It would also be possible for part of an image to be used in creating another, as with the LRR and OLR coaches shown here. Many Midland Red scenes were drawn by 'E.B.M.' who drew the FEDD (page 43 Residential Districts), an attractive drawing but not such an accurate representation of the vehicle.

1914 TS3 OA4560

1916 TS3 OB1111

1919 TS3 OE1127

1920 TS3 OE6156

1920 TS3 OE6165

1920 TS3 OE6196

1922 Garford HA2318

1922 Garford HA2318

1922 TS3 OE7312

1922 TS3 OE7312

1923 S HA2334

1925 FS HA2500

1925 S HA2436

1926 FS HA3528

1927 QC HA3668

1928 QLC HA4835

1928 QL HA3786

1929 M HA4910

1929 MM HA5008

1929 XL HA4966

1929 XL HA4966

1930 QLC HA5136

1930 SRR HA6174

1932 IM4 HA8279

1932 REDD HA8017

1934 DON HA9485

1934 FEDD HA9429

1934 LRR HA9398

1935 OLR AHA612

OLR/LRR artwork hybrid

1936 SON CHA509

1937 SLR CHA998

1943 S3 CHA2

1945 DI HHAI

1946 S6 HHA601

1948 CI KHA302

1950 C2 KHA345

1952 S13 OHA 968

1953 LD8 SHA405

A Brief History

British Electric Traction (BET) used to be one of the major transport providers in the UK, as mighty as Arriva, First and Stagecoach are today. Created to promote tramway development, it invested also in bus operations, and in 1899 it purchased the assets of the failed Birmingham General Omnibus Co Ltd which had around 70 horse buses requiring over 500 horses. BET ordered new horse buses in 1900 and specified that they should be bright red.

The Birmingham & Midland Motor Omnibus Company, Ltd, was registered on 26 November 1904 by Birmingham Motor Express Co Ltd, already operating a small fleet of motorbuses, as a means of raising capital. It failed to attract sufficient interest and instead the directors of BME sold out to BET. Thus by the time BMMO became operational in August 1905, it had also become a subsidiary of British Electric Traction which had put under its wing the various horse and motorbus assets it had gathered in the Birmingham area. Thus, despite 'Motor' in its name and the small number of very unreliable motorbuses – soon abandoned – the new company was actually in charge of 100 horse buses with 1,000 horses. With the financial strength of the BET behind it, BMMO therefore started with a major advantage over most other beginners in the bus business.

BMMO's horse buses were quite unable to compete with the Corporation's new electric tramcars and, indeed, it was then a condition of the licences issued by Birmingham Watch Committee that omnibuses should not operate on tramway routes, so as a new tramway route opened, horse bus service was withdrawn.

The Birmingham network was thus shrinking but new, reliable, motorbuses were introduced from 25 May 1912. These red painted buses, on Tilling-Stevens chassis, carried the BET magnet emblem on their flanks. Further deliveries the following year were the start of an ambitious programme to link up all the towns and villages within a radius of 30 miles of Birmingham. The 1913 buses were the first to carry the fleetname 'MIDLAND' – the Midland "Red" legend had begun.

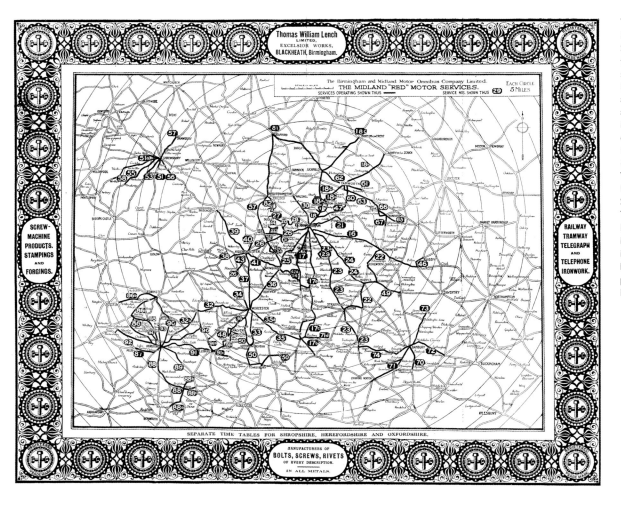

This route map is taken from the Summer 1920 timetable. The scale is shown by circles 5 miles apart. Services are developing in a number of centres outside Birmingham (Hereford, Worcester, Kidderminster, Sutton Coldfield, Tamworth and Banbury, plus an isolated group in Shrewsbury), but there is no presence yet in Leicester.

This 1918 letterhead shows 1914 Tilling Stevens TS3 OA 4560 and lists 5 garages and 3 Enquiry Offices.

A letterhead with 1920 TS3 OE 6165 showing further expansion.

All existing horse bus routes were quickly converted to motorbuses and, during 1913, local services commenced in districts just outside Birmingham. However, on 5 September, Birmingham Corporation opened an electric tramway along the Hagley Road, which was thus placed 'out of bounds' to BMMO buses, and it was obvious that something would have to be done to avoid further conflict between the two parties.

Negotiations led to a highly successful agreement between BMMO and Birmingham Corporation dated 14 February 1914, whereby the company would not compete with the Corporation within the city boundary and the Corporation would not compete with the company outside. BMMO removed its headquarters to its existing Bearwood garage and began to build up a network of services from central Birmingham to points outside the city boundary, fare arrangements giving protection to the Corporation's services.

The outbreak of World War One in 1914 was a major blow to many other companies who had buses, or at least their chassis, requisitioned by the War Office. The military did not initially approve of Tilling-Stevens chassis, however, as its petrol engine did not directly drive the bus through a gearbox but via a dynamo powering a large electric motor. BMMO thus kept its fleet intact and new examples continued to be delivered so it was able to step in when both associated and rival companies had to withdraw facilities. Soon Midland Red vehicles were working in Kidderminster, Worcester, Warwick, Nuneaton and Tamworth.

The War ended in November 1918 and BMMO set about consolidating its wartime gains and expanding into new areas. As O C Power liked to remark, "During those years we were painting the map red." But it was a period of intense competition. Many men had been released from military service with experience of driving and maintaining motor vehicles, war surplus examples at reasonable price being within reach of the ordinary man for once in his lifetime as he received his war gratuity. BMMO, of course, had only begun its outward march from Birmingham at the outset of the War but had the advantage of size and the financial backing of the BET group, which saw the business potential of connecting up towns and picking up fares from the country districts between those towns. BET also now acknowledged the lower risk of bus operation compared with tramways, as buses could be moved from an unprofitable route and used elsewhere, whilst a tramway was a long-term commitment.

It was an era of fearless investment and Traffic Manager Orlando Cecil Power dynamically promoted the company's services. BMMO decided upon a policy of attack and no mileage was dropped as long as a reasonable return could be obtained. Competition would be challenged, and, where practicable, eliminated. Additionally, the company began regular long distance services from Birmingham to coastal resorts in 1921, the first services being from Birmingham to Weston-super-Mare and to Llandudno. An opening to develop long-distance services had come with the railway strike of 1919 when buses were provided at short notice to carry stranded passengers.

One major objective was to establish services in and around Leicester where Midland Red began a determined campaign. This highlighted that the competition was often armed with small, fast, lightweight buses that ran rings around the Midland Red Tilling-Stevens petrol-electrics. Mr Shire, Midland Red's Chief Engineer, was conscious of this shortcoming. Bus manufacturers failed to meet his requirement for vehicles that combined the capacity of the Tillings with the nimbleness of the small 'opposition' buses, so he took the historic decision that the Company would design and build its own buses, badged SOS. These were also supplied to other BET companies, including Northern General Transport where the light, fast and comfortable SOS buses were credited as playing a bigger part in eliminating the competition than any previous strategy. Similarly, the tramways of sister BET companies in the Black Country suffered from independent buses so Midland Red vehicles were sent in to deal with the competition and eventually replaced the trams too.

The big four railway companies had gained powers to operate bus services in 1928 but, instead of entering into wasteful competition, approached major bus companies and bought into them. On 24 April 1930, the Great Western Railway and the London, Midland & Scottish Railway purchased half the ordinary shares of the BMMO company. The most visible change was on the company letterheads where the railway participation became clearly evident.

A few days after the railway investment in the company, BMMO purchased on 30 April 1930 Black & White Motorways Ltd of Cheltenham, one of the principal operators of long distance coach services. Black & White retained its separate identity, however, and its control was shared with two other companies, Bristol Tramways and City of Oxford Motor Services.

1 July 1934 was the first day of a major step towards a nationwide, co-ordinated, coach network, with partners pooling specified services and operating them as an indivisible whole, eliminating wasteful competition. This was the creation of 'Associated Motorways', in which BMMO was an important partner. The focal point was the Black & White coach station at Cheltenham where coaches connected and passengers interchanged.

Among several important purchases in the mid-1930s was Stratford-upon-Avon Blue Motors Ltd, operating under the fleetname Stratford Blue, with whom Midland Red had agreed a working arrangement in September 1932. This delightful company was retained as a subsidiary for many years. The National Bus Company, however, was not keen on small subsidiaries so Stratford Blue was finally absorbed into Midland Red on 1 January 1971.

The outbreak of World War Two in 1939 temporarily halted the company's forward progress as men, some vehicles and even garages were lost to the war effort. There were substantial new demands to serve factories on war work, and carry people who had moved to outlying towns and villages, but new buses were very few. Express services and tours ceased completely and had to be rebuilt from scratch after peace returned in 1945.

The restoration after World War Two of many facilities that had been curtailed, petrol rationing for private car owners, and new housing estates created a temporary demand for increased frequencies and new services. Price inflation and television crippled evening travel demand, however, and led to a steady financial decline from the mid-1950s. Staff shortages began on the platform side but eventually spread to engineering, particularly when the craftsmen who had spent their lives with the company retired.

Replacement staff were hard to get due to the then buoyant car industry and its higher pay. Leyland Leopards and Daimler Fleetlines had to be bought to supplement the falling output of new vehicles from Carlyle Works and production of BMMO buses fell to an uneconomic level, ending in 1970.

The railways' shares in BMMO had passed to the state upon railway nationalisation in 1948. Midland Red had remained under private control with British Electric Traction until the latter sold its British bus interests to the state with effect from 14 March 1968 and the National Bus Company was created to take control over the English and Welsh subsidiaries from 1 January 1969. The company was already in bad shape when the NBC took over. NBC corporate images quickly replaced the Midland Red style, thus ending the subject of this book. Firstly there was the imposition of white 'National' coach livery for all subsidiaries and then, from autumn 1972, the bland poppy red with even blander lettering for the buses. It only remains to refer to the sale by NBC of the lucrative Black Country operations to the West Midlands PTE in 1973, and the division of Midland Red into several smaller companies from 5 September 1981. These smaller companies were subsequently privatised and have vanished into the new large groups.

The coach station at Cheltenham with Midland Red LRR class AHA 608 prominent. *Courtesy Colin Martin*

ORLANDO CECIL POWER JP

Orlando Cecil Power was born at King's Heath in 1879. He left school at 14 and initially worked in a printing firm but, wanting to be a journalist, became Private Secretary to the United States Consul in Birmingham, George F Parker, who was a prominent US journalist and had been Secretary to President Grover Cleveland. Power hoped to return to the USA with Parker, but Parker was asked to stay on in the UK so Power took another direction.

He joined the British Electric Traction's Birmingham area horse bus subsidiaries, where his career was meteoric. He was appointed Secretary of the Birmingham General Omnibus Company when its assets were purchased by BET in 1899, and became traffic manager in 1902 at the age of 23. In the same year, he also became Manager of the horse bus department of the Birmingham Tramway Company when that was acquired by BET, and the Birmingham Motor Express was taken over, bringing fledgling motorbuses under his wing too.

Power became Traffic Manager of the new BMMO Company in 1904. In 1908 he was also appointed Traffic and Claims Manager of the Birmingham and Midland Tramways' Joint Committee, which controlled the whole of the Black Country Tramways, the Kidderminster and Stourport Tramways, and the greater part of the City of Birmingham Tramways Company's lines which had not been taken over by the Birmingham Corporation. As a result, he had the unique experience of being concerned at the same time with horse omnibuses, motor omnibuses, horse trams, steam trams, overhead electric trams, accumulator electric trams, cable trams and other activities.

OCP, as he became known, was a man who found seven days barely sufficient to complete a week, and who displayed ability, thoroughness, courtesy and a genial personality in everything he did. The Chief Constable of Birmingham later stated that he and OCP had never had a misunderstanding during over 33 years of working together.

OCP liked to say that he had done a very great deal towards "painting the map red." "We have had the satisfaction, and very real it is, of opening up the country for a lot of people who were not able to travel before," he said. "And, incidentally, we have almost revolutionised some of the smaller towns in the district, such as Bromsgrove, Worcester, Kidderminster, Shrewsbury and Hereford. We take many thousands of people to those places, and have turned them from quiet, old-fashioned centres into busy towns and naturally most of the people we take spend money while there. We also fetch the country people in from the surrounding districts on market days, which is a very great convenience and saving to them."

From 1912, when motorbuses were reintroduced, OCP shared day-to-day management and development of the company with Chief Engineer Wyndham Shire. Surprisingly, there was no general manager for many years, the two divisions of Midland Red working separately under these great personalities who did not always see eye-to-eye. OCP was described in a BET publication as "a character of singular force and originality", with "a breezy and delightful personality". Such was his reputation that, among his other activities, were directorships of several other BET subsidiaries including Black and White Motorways, Trent Motor Traction, Potteries Motor Traction and Standerwick.

In contrast to Shire, Power was an accessible man. He held meetings with his conductors and other staff, and he was available for those who had reason to see him. His personality endeared him to the travelling public. The newly promoted Resident Inspector at Redditch in 1914 received a letter from OCP telling him to treat his own area as if he were the sole proprietor. He saw the benefit of a single trade union to negotiate on behalf of the platform staff, and he authorised the introduction of the staff magazine as early as 1932. On the retirement of a long-serving driver in 1938 he gave "one of his usual humorous speeches with reminiscences of the old horse bus days".

Upon his appointment as a Justice of the Peace in 1933, the Birmingham Post described him as "One of the most popular and well-known public men in the Midlands". No wonder Shire disliked him!

OCP died suddenly at a meeting of the Public Transport Association in London in 1943, still in post as Traffic Manager. Modern Transport reported that he had worked 44 Easter Mondays in a row supervising operations in the centre of Birmingham. The Chairman of the Birmingham Watch Committee referred to the many years they had been associated in the public work of the City and said that "I wish that all the people I have met in public life had the same honesty of purpose, ability and conceptions of public duty which you have displayed in the many relations I have had with you".

The Power Era Begins

The first timetable for buses only in Birmingham is thought to have been one issued in May 1903 by the BET, giving details of the horse bus services of the Birmingham and Midland Tramways, of which the Traffic Manager was OC Power. 10,000 were issued free, the cost being covered by advertisements.

The first official Midland Red timetable booklet was issued free in March 1914. This was called the 'Midland Motor Omnibus Guide' and copies were available in 'Please Take One' boxes on the buses. It had 24 pages covering 16 bus services, together with details of the

Kinver tram services, the Tramway Parcels Express, Motor Omnibuses for Private Hire and the Horse Contract department. Further editions were published in April and May. From June 1914, publication was taken over by the Tram Guides Company. Now called the Motor Bus Guide, it initially cost 1d and included details of Birmingham Corporation buses operating from the Selly Oak tram terminus to Rednal and Rubery. This continued to be published monthly until 1924, though Midland Red resumed publishing its own timetable in April 1919.

Right: An extract from a timetable, part of a 'Tramway Guide between Birmingham and the Black Country', published by the Birmingham and Midland Tramways Joint Committee. It was issued after the introduction of the Birmingham-Walsall service on 24 December 1913 but before the October 1914 takeover of Tennant Street and certain services by Birmingham Corporation.

Above right: The 1920 timetable reveals the rapid expansion to Tamworth, Nuneaton, Banbury, Hereford, Wolverhampton and Bromsgrove with 1919 TS3 OE1127 shown on the cover. The BET insignia was replaced after the first delivery of buses by the MIDLAND fleetname, leading to the Midland 'Red' trading name.

1912 Tilling-Stevens TTA1 double-decker O 8208, in red and black livery with BET magnet and wheel insignia, is posed with Chief Engineer Wyndham Shire sitting at the rear of the upper deck. Mr Shire's choice of the Tilling-Stevens petrol-electric chassis, with its absence of gears, made the transition from horses to motorbuses much easier for drivers. *BMMO*

Single-deckers were red with black mudguards and silver roof. Those built before 1927 were lined out in black with panel edges picked out in gold. This animated view shows Tilling-Stevens TS3 OE 6189 with the style of body introduced in 1920, built in this case to BMMO's design by BRCW. Front destination boards showed the ultimate destinations of the bus service in each direction, while the via points were shown on the side, along with the service number. At this time, the destination board lettering was generally black although some via boards were red. The Birmingham – Coleshill service was numbered 21 at this time, major service renumbering taking place in April 1925 and February 1928. *BMMO, courtesy of Kithead Trust*

A 1921 poster showing a Birmingham to Malvern bus, a forerunner of the famous 144, with a collage of river boats, castles and country houses to be seen on the way. *Courtesy Kithead Trust*

Painting The Map Red

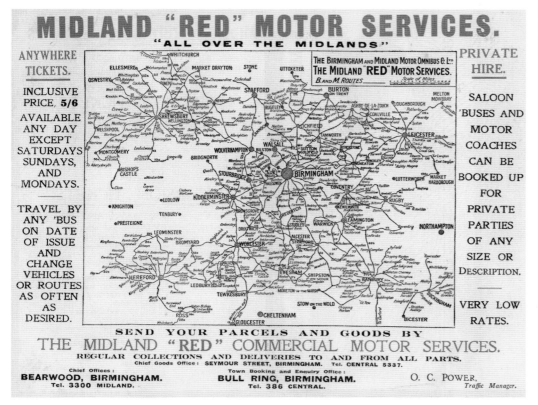

A map from around 1922. The network is nearly in place, but there are notable gaps around Ludlow and Northampton.

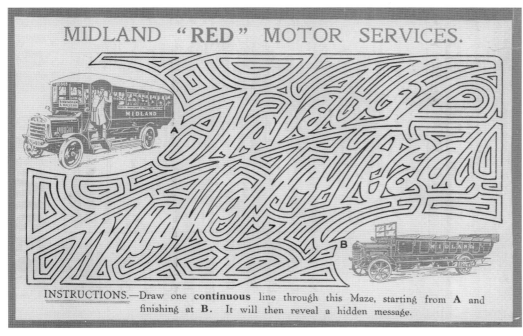

The reverse of the 1922 map shows a Tilling Stevens bus and charabanc. The hidden message reads "Travel by Midland Red". The leaflet offers discounts on the principal routes to Birmingham and discount tickets for regular travellers.

PIONEERING THE "LONG-DISTANCE" BUS IN 1919

J.E.Dutton was a conductor at Bearwood from 1919, becoming an Inspector in 1937 and then Garage Traffic Assistant. He later wrote of his experiences during the Rail strike in 1919, when long-distance bus services were unknown.

"It was in August 1919, and a Railway Strike was in progress. I was working a Coventry "Spare" and at about 6 o'clock I was approached by the Traffic Manager, Mr. O. C. Power, and asked if I would do him a favour. I said I would if I could. He asked me would anybody worry if I stayed out all night! I told him I was in apartments and everything would be all right.

The "Governor" said he had a party who had been travelling the Battle-Fields of France. They were stranded in Birmingham and wanted to get back to Shrewsbury. Could I take them and drop them at points nearest their homes. I got a fresh Driver and was told to work my own way back next morning. Whilst waiting for the return, I was approached by a gentleman enquiring where I was going. After telling him "Birmingham", he asked me could I take a party to Liverpool as they were stranded, and were to appear on the theatre-stage there (The D'Oyley Carte Opera Company). I got through to Bearwood explaining the position to the "Governor". I was asked "Could I do the trip, and did I know the way? I told him I knew all the roads in that direction as I had worked around that way with a Company who afterwards became absorbed into the Potteries Electric Traction, but I should want another Driver as mine did not want to go. A Driver was sent to me and I was told what to charge the passengers for the bus, stay for lunch at Chester, then proceed to Birkenhead and put up at the Woodside Hotel for the night, working my way back next morning.

I was informed at Birkenhead that a boat had arrived from America and I went to see what I could do; but was told a skeleton rail service was running to Birmingham. I found out that there was a load of passengers who wanted to go to London, so I advised the Company and was told to take them and charge them £5 a head, which they accepted. I left at 9.30 a.m. with about 26 passengers.

When I got to Moxley I was met by Inspector Bond and I was told that my Driver would be relieved, and I could carry on to London. A Driver Butler was to take me on and I was to pull up at Fenny Stratford and supply my passengers with lunch at the expense of the Company.

We arrived in London at about 8.30 pm and put up at Tillings Garage for the night. The next morning I went along to Euston Station hoping to get a load for Birmingham. With success I got a load, landing in Birmingham about 5 pm. When I got back to the Garage I found I was booked up for London again next day! On arriving in London with a load for the second time I found that the Railway had started a skeleton service. Using my "head", I stayed outside a Y.M.C.A. hostel for the night, and by exerting a bit of pressure on passengers awaiting for trains, I succeeded in getting together about 20 passengers for Coventry and Birmingham. This was a bit of a surprise to Mr. O. C. Power, who, when I got back wanted to know how I had managed it! I told him by a bit of cheek, and with the help of my Driver Albert Petty!"

Early coaching days with a Tilling-Stevens TS3 char-a-banc. These had a similar livery to buses but the relief was reversed, i.e. the lining was gold with black mouldings. Unfortunately the photo film often used at the time made the red look black so the full effect of the livery is lost. OK 1310 had a Startin 32-seat body and dated from 1922, being seen on a trip to Matlock Bath that year. *E V Trigg. The Transport Museum, Wythall, collection*

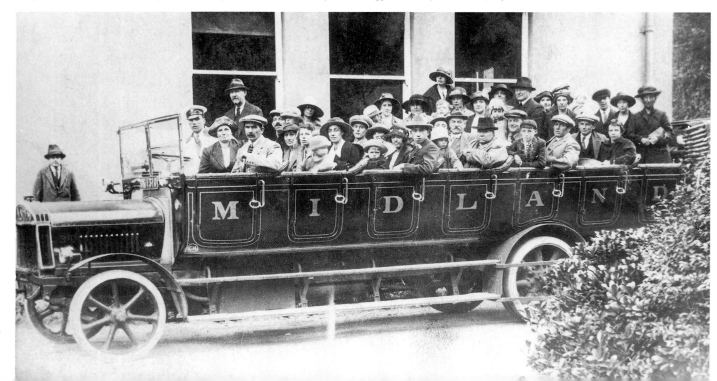

Experiments with lighter Ford and Garford vehicles included two of these dinky 1921 British-built Model T Ford 11-seat char-a-bancs with sign writing unique to them. They were sold after only three years but proved to Mr Shire the benefits of a reliable, straightforward design. *The Transport Museum, Wythall collection*

LOFTUS GEORGE WYNDHAM SHIRE

L G Wyndham Shire was Chief Engineer of Midland Red from 1912 until 1940. He was a distinguished engineer who made outstanding contributions in vehicle design and methods of operational maintenance.

Shire gained his technical education at the City and Guilds Institute and then worked for a short time in the maintenance shops of the Croydon trams.

When BMMO withdrew all its motorbuses in 1907, BET sent six of them to Deal in Kent where it was felt that their operation may be possible. Shire was appointed manager and engineer of Deal and District Motor Services and, as a 'hands-on' engineer, worked all hours of the day. There was no manufacturer's service department – he had to make the parts himself. He was rarely in his office, but in the pit or creating parts on the workbench. His unflagging commitment kept the buses going and this was recognised. When BMMO reintroduced motorbuses, Shire was recruited from Deal to become Chief Engineer, running the day-to-day management of the company jointly with O C Power.

Shire disliked the bus bodies on offer from manufacturers and designed his own lightweight 'no frills' single-decker. Faced with considerable competition after World War One, he wanted buses with the capacity of the existing Tilling-Stevens but with greatly improved performance. He obtained permission from his directors to design and build his own vehicles, an example of his forcefulness and determination. The result was a simple design with a reliable, efficient engine and a lightweight body.

He trained many engineers who went on to senior levels in the industry, of which the following three are typical. **Eric Ottaway** was recruited in 1925 from the Sunbeam Motor Car Company in Wolverhampton, a leading motorsport manufacturer with successes in the French Grand Prix and at Le Mans. Sunbeam were obtaining maximum power and speed from their engines and a bright junior engineer at Sunbeam would have been a good recruit. Ottaway joined Midland Red as Assistant Engineer in Charge of Rolling Stock in 1925 just as SOS production started, leaving in 1929 to join London General, becoming Chief Engineer of London Transport's Chiswick Works in 1940. **William Semmons** was BMMO's Experimental Engineer, including close involvement in the evolution of the company's diesel engine. This brought him into contact with AEC, who supplied the engines for the first SOS diesel buses, and he was headhunted by that manufacturer to further develop its engines, among other things. **Seymour Charles Vince** travelled in the opposite direction. He had a succession of technical managerial positions in London General and the replacing London Transport. He joined Midland Red in 1938 as an Assistant Engineer. When General Manager Donald Sinclair introduced his new management team in 1946, Vince became Chief Engineer. He left in 1955, having been appointed Chief Engineer of the BET Federation.

Sadly, Mr Shire was described as an eccentric, vain and difficult man, characteristics exacerbated no doubt by the frustrations of wartime impositions on the company. He retired in 1940 at the early age, for those times, of only 55.

This prototype double-decker on a Tilling-Stevens TS3 chassis converted to forward control was completed in 1922. It was very unusual in adopting a front entrance and staircase at a time when double-deckers normally had entrances and open staircases at the back. Imagination seems to have run out before thinking of the poor old driver, however! *BMMO, courtesy The Kithead Trust*

55 more were produced to an improved design between 1922 and 1924 on Tilling-Stevens chassis, either new or used, or built up from parts. The driver now sat in an enclosed cab and the prototype was similarly improved. Like the earlier double-deckers, the upper deck was painted black. Bearwood, Leicester and Worcester received permanent allocations of these double-deckers although other garages would borrow them and in time gained them in small numbers on their allocations. *BMMO*

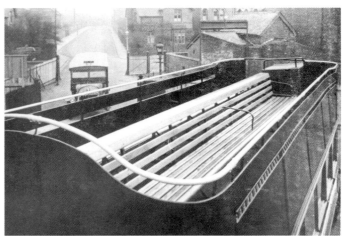

The upper deck seats were arranged longitudinally with the passengers sitting back to back, enabling a hump in the lower saloon roof to give headroom for passengers accessing seats. Seating capacity was 29 downstairs and 22 on top. *BMMO*

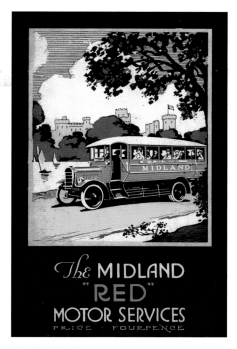

Front and back covers of a six-page leaflet from 1923/4 which encouraged tours for private parties and circular tours from Birmingham by ordinary service buses. The leaflet shows one of the first SOS 'Standards', 1923 HA 2334, with 1922 Garford HA 2318. The leaflet claims the largest pleasure fleet in the country and stresses that 'All our Pleasure Vehicles are now fitted with giant pneumatic tyres'. Twelve circular tours from Birmingham are suggested, ranging from a 48 mile round trip to Warwick, to a 150 mile round trip to Llangollen. Midland Red would organise the entire trip using first class caterers at all destinations.

The 1924 Guide to the company shows a Tilling Stevens TS3 single-decker on route 23 to Shipston, a two and a half hour journey from Birmingham via Henley and Stratford.

The company's own chassis were known as SOS, a patent filed by Shire in 1924 refers to 'Superior Omnibus Specification'. Chief Engineer Mr Shire would simply say "I'll leave it to you to interpret the initials", encouraging the view that the first S stood for Shire's! It was part of Shire's style to be annoyingly vague! A proportion of SOS vehicles were turned out as char-a-bancs. There was no centre gangway in a true char-a-banc (literally French for wagon with benches), each row of seats being accessed by individual doors. Unlike the Tilling charas which had doors on both sides, the SOS vehicles had nearside doors only. HA 2353 dated from 1923 and, like other early SOS vehicles, had a chassis frame constructed by Tilling with BMMO features and fittings. Davidson built the 32-seat coachwork. *BMMO*

The first long-distance service was between Birmingham and Weston-super-Mare, inaugurated on 7 May 1921, followed by a service to Llandudno, commenced on 6 June. They originally had service numbers 200 and 201. Standard single-deckers were normally employed but they were blessed with cushion seats; wooden seats were usual until 1922. This 1923 scene in Seymour Street, Birmingham, shows a very busy day with one of the company's more unusual vehicles assisting. Conductors were always carried and one can be seen loading luggage on the vehicle behind, ladders being kept at terminals and major interchange points. Midland Red advertising can be seen in the background. E 1843 was ex-North Warwickshire Motor Omnibus & Traction Co Ltd, another company with a BET interest, which found itself in trouble. Midland Red buses started to work what remained of its network of services out of Nuneaton and Twogates, near Tamworth from 1 February 1918. Eight Tilling-Stevens double and single-deck vehicles were added to stock from this operator and some worked for many years with their new owner. E 1843 received this char-a-banc body in 1919, one of several purchased by BMMO around this time for fitting to Tilling chassis, in this case by Tillotson. Body exchanging was a feature of this period, bodies being lifted for overhauls which were required frequently. *BMMO/ The Transport Museum, Wythall*

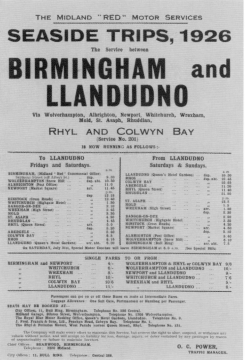

Not much difference once the passengers reached Llandudno as early SOS vehicles were also supplied to other operators in the BET empire, including the Llandudno Coaching & Carriage Co Ltd, trading as Royal Blue. The record year for SOS production was 1928 when 349 buses and 30 coaches were produced, of which around half were for other operators. Nearly all SOS vehicles had bodies built to Midland Red's design irrespective of operator. This advert for Royal Blue appeared in Midland Red's 1930 Holiday Tours booklet. There were big changes in North Wales after the railways invested in the various bus companies, one consequence being the 1931 absorption of Royal Blue into Crosville.

All Over The Midlands

OSCAR FIDOE

Oscar Fidoe served 38 years with Midland Red and predecessor between 1900 and 1937, and is typical of the front line staff forming the bedrock of the company. He started as a horse-bus conductor in Birmingham and was then given charge of charabancs running to Coleshill and Stourbridge. When the company began to expand in 1914 he suggested mid-Warwickshire and was given responsibility for developing services there. He ran the first BMMO bus based in Warwick, and then three services between Leamington and Coventry. He became Resident Inspector at Leamington in charge of six men – by the time he retired there were 180. He was an enthusiastic cyclist in his spare time and developed a wide knowledge of the area which he used in developing bus services. In particular, it was Inspector Fidoe who developed and popularised the tours of the Shakespeare country in the 1920s.

Lower left A network was established in Leicester by 1922 and this district guide detailed the services soon offered. The Tilling-Stevens TS3 bus OE 6182 of 1920 has Midland Red cast on the radiator.

Below Stratford-on-Avon and 'Shakespeare Land' has always been a popular destination. Regular day tours were run from Leamington from the 1920s.

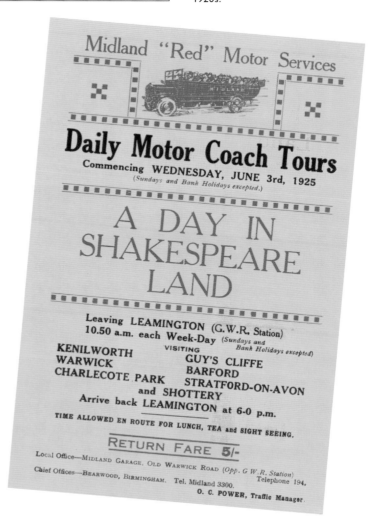

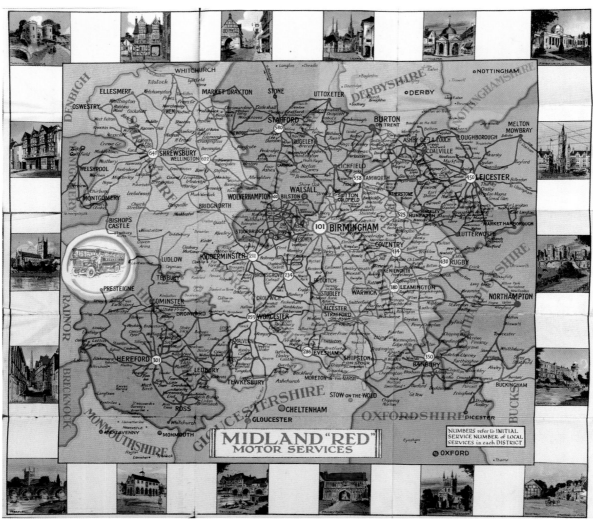

This 1927 map was in full colour and included drawings of interesting destinations. The numbers shown in the principal towns and cities are the beginning of the block of local service numbers allocated to those places. Service renumbering would take place in 1928.

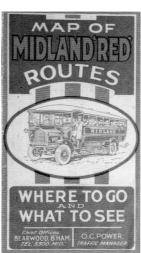
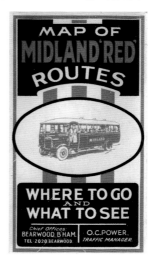

A collection of route map covers from the later 1920s.

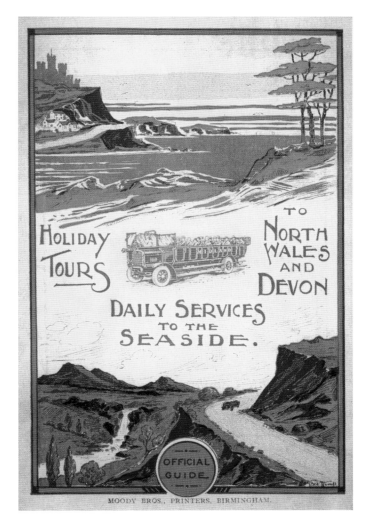

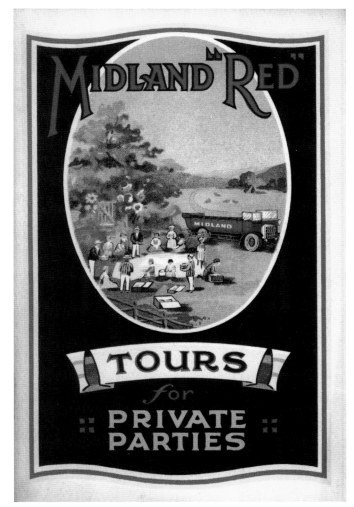

Following a 1925 prototype, forward control SOS vehicles entered production in 1926 in both char-a-banc and bus versions (see pages 4 and 6), classified FS for Forward Steering. The former were used on the company's first coach cruises but separating the driver in his own cab from passengers was found to be unsatisfactory for touring. Future touring coaches therefore reverted to normal control, beginning with the QC models that, together with the QLCs, operated the Holiday Tours until the mid 1930s. The FS charas were soon rebodied as buses. The first Holiday Tours were to Devon in 1927, using FS char-a-bancs. North Wales tours were soon added. Special mention was made in the programme of the pneumatic tyres of the FS. A five-day tour to Glorious Devon cost £7 17 shillings and 6 pence (£7.87½p) including all costs of five-star hotels. Central Wales, East Anglia, London and the South Coast became additional holiday destinations.

The 1927 model was the Q (Queen) class that carried a simplified livery with a black line beneath the windows and gold lining, exemplified by HA 3643. By this time, in addition to the destination boards, stencils were in use for displaying the service numbers. *BMMO, courtesy of Kithead Trust*

Booklets were published in the 1920s describing destinations for trips by service bus, and suggesting circular tours. These were aimed at commercial travellers as well as day-trippers and tourists.

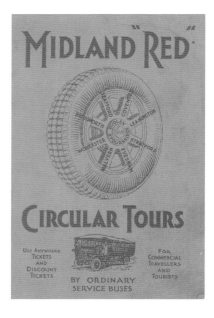

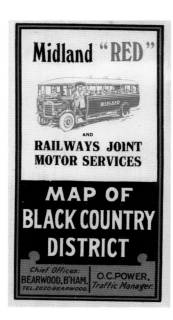

A further livery adjustment introduced on the 1928 QL buses was the partially underlined fleetname. Here is the style on 1929 M (for Madam) HA 4948 under a rather grand sign at Hereford. The Madam, as may be implied by the name, introduced a substantial improvement in passenger comfort as well as a more modern appearance, particularly the curved side panels. *J F Higham, courtesy Alan B Cross*

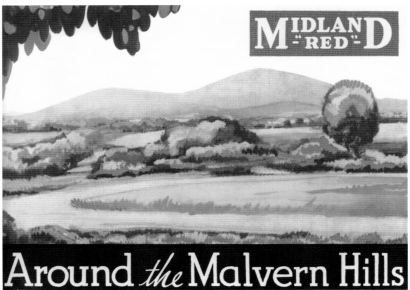

Leaflets promoted Malvern and its hills to travellers, and Midland Red services to those who were already there. The advertisement (right) comes from a local guide to the town.

Over the Hills and Far Away

Mr Shire designed a new fleet of touring char-a-bancs, entering service between 1927 and 1930. These benefited from pneumatic tyres in tandem with much improved comfort within. Mr Power's team rigorously exploited the new opportunities to open up the countryside and visit more distant places. Romantic drawings exploited the dream that the rural idyll of Merrie England, and Merrie Wales too, was just around the corner and Midland Red knew where to find it. Bonnie Scotland would follow.

Glass positive slides were used to promote holiday tours and trips for private parties. Lantern Lectures on "Beauty Spots of the Midland 'Red' Country" were offered to organisations wanting to arrange outings. Lecture notes were provided with the slides. The 1928 timetables offered those near Birmingham a lecturer, Mr John Hingeley, together with a soloist and pianist if required! Over 200 lectures were given over the winter season.

1930 QLC HA 5138 is seen touring Dartmoor. These ancient glass positives were hand coloured for Midland Red between around 1920 and 1930 and must have created quite an impression in an era when movies were still silent and monochrome. *The Transport Museum, Wythall, archive*

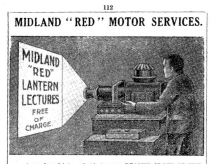

112

MIDLAND "RED" MOTOR SERVICES.

MIDLAND "RED" LANTERN LECTURES FREE OF CHARGE.

A number of interesting lectures on BEAUTY SPOTS OF THE MIDLAND "RED" COUNTRY have now been compiled for which lantern slides, complete with descriptive readings, can be obtained on loan.

1. Beauty Spots of the Midlands.
2. Historic Towns and Picturesque Villages.
3. Rambles in Leafy Warwickshire.
4. Along Worcestershire Ways.
5. The Severn from Shrewsbury to Tewkesbury.
6. Shrines of Saints and Celebrities.
7. Highways and Byways of the Borderland.
8. A Gossip about Birmingham.

The slides are lent free of charge, but an undertaking must be given that they will be carefully handled and returned the day after the lecture is given.

At places within convenient reach of Birmingham, the Midland "Red" Special Lecturer, Mr. John Hingeley, will attend, if desired, and lantern, screen and Operator will be supplied free of charge.

Arrangements can also be made for a Soloist and Pianist to be sent if required.

Send a post card to the Chief Office, or telephone "Midland 3300" (Publicity Department), and ask for "Application for Lecture" Form.

Secretaries of Clubs, Societies or Organisations of any kind are asked to communicate as quickly as possible, as numerous dates are already filled.

CHIEF OFFICES :— Bearwood, Birmingham. Tel. 3300 Midland.

O. C. POWER, Traffic Manager.

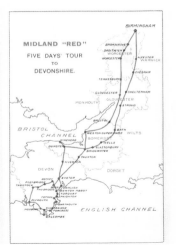

Midland "Red" Motor Services.

FIVE DAYS' TOUR
TO GLORIOUS DEVON
FROM BIRMINGHAM.

A TOUR OF OVER 565 MILES.

By Midland "Red."

Visiting:—
Bath, Wells, Bridgwater, Taunton, Exeter, Dawlish, Teignmouth, Torquay, Paignton, Bovey Tracey, Manaton, Bickey Falls, Two Bridges, Princetown, Tavistock, Plymouth, Kingsbridge, Salcombe, Tor Cross, Dartmouth, Totnes, Tiverton, Minehead, Weston-Super-Mare, Gloucester.

All-weather Super Motor Coach de Luxe, with pneumatic tyres, leaving the Bull Ring at 8.30 a.m. every Monday from June 13th to July 25th, and from September 5th to 19th inclusive, returning to Birmingham on Friday.

INCLUSIVE FARE 7 Guineas.

Fare includes all First-class Hotel accommodation, Dinner, Bed, Breakfast, Lunch, and all gratuities.

ITINERARY.

1st Day.—Leave Birmingham 8.30 a.m., Alcester, Evesham, Cheltenham, Stroud, Bath (lunch), Wells, Glastonbury, Bridgwater, Taunton, arrive about 6.30 p.m. (dinner, bed, and breakfast).

2nd Day.—Leave Taunton 9.30 a.m., Collumpton, Exeter, Dawlish, Teignmouth, Newton Abbot, Torquay, Paignton (lunch, dinner, bed, and breakfast), arrive about 1 p.m.

3

The Holiday Tours were successful and further tours were rapidly introduced. The map in the 1930 booklet revealed that they now covered most of Wales and southern England.

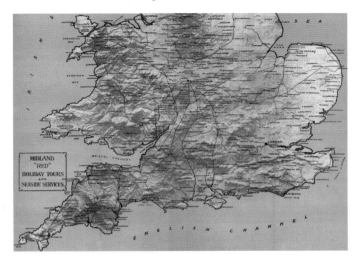

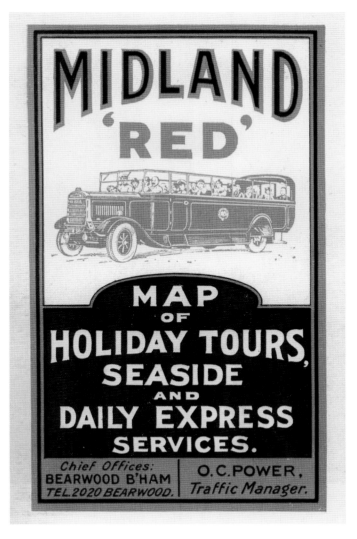

Touring coach passengers continued to travel in the open, unless the hood was raised. The QC and QLC (Q and QL Coach) models of 1927-30 had permanent glass side windows in polished frames and a fixed rear dome that meant the driver could slide the hood into place much more easily than hitherto, aided by the centre gangway now provided. Long distance, private hire and excursion drivers wore white coats. Note the elegant garter monogram instead of fleetnames. HA 3667 is at Lower Lode, near Tewkesbury. *E V Trigg/ The Transport Museum, Wythall collection*

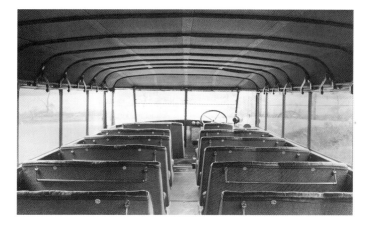

The rather claustrophobic interior of the QC and QLC coaches when the hood was in use, no doubt particularly foggy if the Midland Red cigarettes in the advert, from 1929, were popular. *BMMO, courtesy Kithead Trust*

WILLS'S
MIDLAND RED
TOBACCO
PER 10½d OZ.
STRAIGHT CUT VIRGINIA

Whilst on a tobacco theme, this ashtray dates from 1928 and shows the familiar illustration of the FS bus with a Birmingham destination and side board reading 'To All Parts of the Midlands'. It was produced for a reception held in The Guildhall, Worcester in 1928 to mark the signing of the "Worcester Agreement" by which Midland Red buses took over operation of local services in the city on behalf of the Corporation, replacing its trams. A cigarette case showing the same bus is also known to have existed.

Day and half-day trips continued to increase in popularity. A delightful view showing coachmen promoting Cotswold tours. *Roger Torode collection*

Midland Red style moved to another level with the elegant and imposing SOS QLC tour coaches of 1929-30. HA 5139 is seen on tour. *E V Trigg collection*

Midland Red built up a strong business in private tours and could cater 'for parties of any size or description'. The early 1920s leaflets for individual tours shown opposite developed into an annual booklet given to anyone enquiring about arranging a trip. The 1930 edition lists 164 day tours and 15 Sunday Morning Runs.

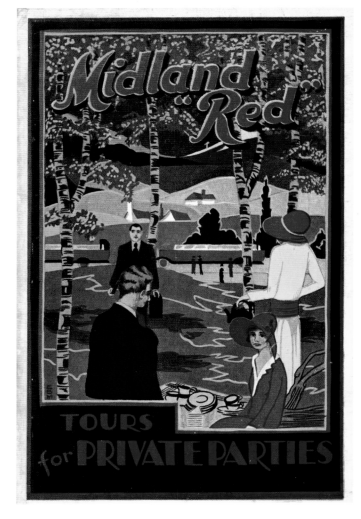

One of a series of 1920s leaflets promoting tours for private parties. Tour number 12 to Llangollen was the most ambitious, a 150 mile round trip through north Wales.

A new fleet of 50 long distance express coaches, introducing a red and maroon livery for such vehicles, was introduced in 1929. Initially known as the XL (Excel) class, they did not excel – the 30-seat bodies were too heavy for the chassis. Here is HA 4957 in original XL form, lettered for the service to Weston-super-Mare. *BMMO/ courtesy of Kithead Trust*

The XL vehicles were given new bus bodies to form MM class six-cylinder engined-buses. Beefier chassis were built for the coach bodies to form the RR (Rolls Royce) class. The reference to the famous car manufacturer does not refer to any of its parts being employed, simply Chief Engineer Mr Shire's ambition for similar quality. HA 4999 is seen at Cheltenham with RR chassis and the roller destination blind, the RR class being the first to enjoy this luxury! The registrations remained with the bodies rather than the chassis, a practice that had been technically illegal since 1921.
Malcolm Keeley collection

LONG DISTANCE SERVICES

MIDLAND RED
AND RAILWAYS JOINT MOTOR SERVICES

SERVICE R
BIRMINGHAM & PAIGNTON

Via BRISTOL, EXETER, TEIGNMOUTH & TORQUAY
(Joint Service with Greyhound Motors Limited)

Time Table operative from SEPTEMBER 28th, 1931, until
WHITSUNTIDE, 1932 (except December 25th).

MIDLAND RED

SERVICE "J"
BIRMINGHAM
& LONDON

A photograph taken at the depot of Midland Red omnibuses at Digbeth, Birmingham, on Saturday

When in BIRMINGHAM
Patronise the

MIDLAND RED
CAFE

DIGBETH.

LUNCHEONS
TEAS
BUFFET

Cigarettes, Minerals, Ices, etc.

ENTRANCE:—INSIDE THE
MIDLAND "RED" COACH STATION,
DIGBETH.

:: OPEN ALL DAY ::
WEEKDAYS and SUNDAYS

One Step from Coach to Cafe!

In the recession-hit 1930s, even Digbeth in Birmingham could be made to feel glamorous as a gateway to other places! It opened in 1929.

Right This elegant garter motif graced coaches delivered between 1927 and 1939. It was also applied to the rears of service buses built over the same period, making a final appearance on the S6 vehicles of 1946-7. It also appeared below the windscreens of front engine buses delivered between 1934 and 1945.

BIDFORD CHURCH

MIDLAND "RED"

AND

RAILWAYS JOINT
MOTOR SERVICES
ILLUSTRATED GUIDE

The 1930 Illustrated Guide showed a QL bus in the picturesque village of Bidford, Warwickshire. The wording 'and railways Joint' has been added since the same cover was used the previous year, following the purchase of shares in Midland Red by the Railway companies. This 176 page booklet is a gazetteer to the Midlands with descriptions of towns, villages and countryside, and advice on how to get there by Midland Red.

Bidford was served by the very lengthy X91 service.

MIDLAND "RED"
and Railways Joint Motor Services.

SERVICE No.
X91

Leicester,
The Malverns and
Hereford,

(Via NUNEATON, COVENTRY, LEAMINGTON SPA, STRATFORD-ON-AVON, EVESHAM, WORCESTER and LEDBURY.)

MONDAY, MAY 18th, 1931,
and until further notice.

MIDLAND "RED"
AND RAILWAYS
Joint Motor Services
·LEICESTER DISTRICT·
ILLUSTRATED GUIDE

This Leicester area guide with a nice rendition of an IM4 replaced an earlier booklet showing a similar but less clearly-drawn scene with an FS in this location.

Handbills from 1930 showing services in the Hereford and Malvern areas.

The service between Northampton and Birmingham was introduced on 31 May 1929. This was extended westwards to Shrewsbury from 12 April 1930. The fondly remembered X96, as it was known, was one of the longest stage carriage routes in the country with around 150 fare stages over the 101 miles. 1932 IM4 (Improved Madam 4-cylinder engine) HA 8246 demonstrates the EXPRESS sign used for a period. The asymmetric look of Mr Shire's creations is well demonstrated here. *BMMO*

You could change at Shrewsbury onto buses serving the picturesque A49 and its fine small towns such as Ludlow and Church Stretton, which both justified company promotional leaflets.

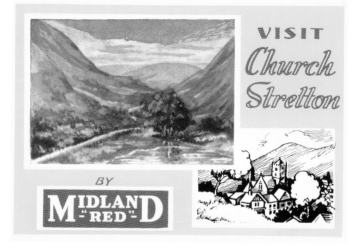

Fresh leaflets were issued throughout the year encouraging travel to local attractions and reflecting the changing scenery through the seasons of the year. Special services for anglers, and individual 1930s leaflets for destinations that could be reached by service buses are shown here.

The Variety Tours booklets were published each year suggesting trips that could be made throughout the Midlands by ordinary service buses. The 1938 edition had 92 pages with detailed itineraries for 204 day trips from 16 starting points across the Midlands. It also had a gazetteer of towns and villages served by Midland Red, with suggested country walks and places of interest. Maps and route information were given for each suggestion.

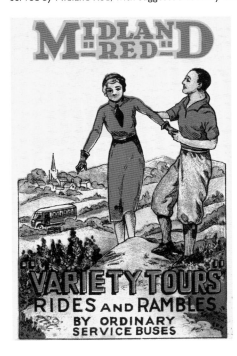

A 1933 calendar showing 1929 XL HA 4966 and 1932 IM4 HA 8279.

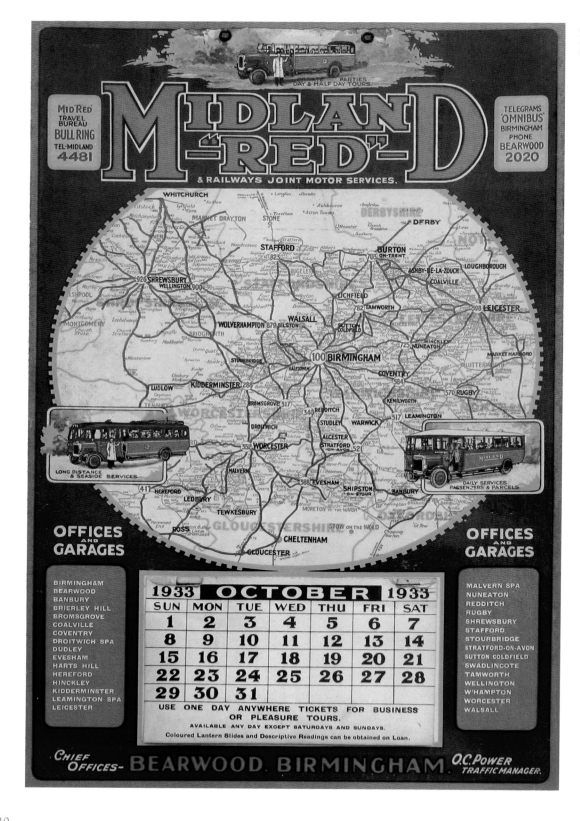

Road Traffic Act Consolidation

The need to increase the number of seats per bus, particularly after the Road Traffic Act 1930 imposed restrictions on the number of standees, brought the reintroduction of double-deckers. A 48-seat (22 up, 26 down) prototype was produced in 1931, HA 7329, bodied by Short Bros.. This was followed in 1932-3 by 50 production vehicles, HA 8001-50, of improved design accommodating four more passengers upstairs. They were bodied by no less than four coachbuilders, Short, Eastern Counties, Brush and Metro-Cammell, the latter having metal frames. They became known as the REDD class (Rear Entrance Double-Decker), and their livery introduced cream relief bands for double-decker buses. These were the first service buses to supplement the stencil numbers with roller destination blinds, previously only fitted to the RR coaches. One of the services they were used on was the 144 with HA 8004 seen here at work at Rose Bank gardens, Great Malvern. *R T Wilson/ The Transport Museum, Wythall*

The company's preference for forward entrance buses resurfaced after just one batch of the rear-entrance double-deckers. After a 1933 prototype with somewhat strange frontal appearance, well over three hundred 56-seat double-deckers were built to this general arrangement between 1934 and the outbreak of World War Two in 1939 and classified FEDD (Front Entrance Double-Decker). The first 50 production FEDDs, with HA registrations, carried Short Bros bodies. HA 9401 at Malvern. *The Transport Museum, Wythall, collection*

THE HAPPY HOLIDAY WAY!

DAILY TRIPS & TOURS
All over the Midlands

Official Time Table and Map, Price 2d.
Buy the Popular Midland "Red" Summer Guide
"Helps to Happy Holidays" Price 6d.
Over 900 pages of good reading and pictures.
Descriptive Notes of Holiday Tours, 2, 5, 6, 7 and 12 days.
Gazetteer of Midland "Red" Country.

DAILY SERVICE TO LONDON
Leave Stratford-on-Avon 9-0 a.m.   Return Fare 14/6

Booking & Enquiry Offices:
STRATFORD BLUE, "Red Lion" Bus Station
(Parcels Office)   Tel. Stratford-on-Avon 2307
BRIDGE STREET (Tel. Stratford-upon-Avon 2237)
SEND YOUR PARCELS BY BUS.

Chief Offices:
BIRMINGHAM.
Tel. Bearwood 2020.

LEAMINGTON OFFICES:
Old Warwick Road & The Parade.
Tel. 194

O. C. POWER,
TRAFFIC MANAGER.

The next 135 FEDDs, dating from 1935-6 and with BHA registration numbers, carried Metro-Cammell metal-framed bodies; a further 15 were built but diverted to associated company Trent. These were the last buses to be built with petrol engines, the company's own K-type 8 litre diesel engine becoming available soon after. The fine quality of the Metro-Cammell bodies meant it was worth the company converting them to diesel between 1942 and 1947 with AEC 7.7 or BMMO K engines. *Metro-Cammell*

The interiors of these FEDDs (below left) featured this striking Art Deco moquette (*opposite page*).

This publication from the mid-1930s described the qualities of the residential areas around Midland Red's centres of operation, to encourage regular commuter travel by bus. The suburbs of Birmingham are described in glowing terms, together with the residential advantages of Leamington, Leicester, Rugby, Worcester, Wolverhampton, Coventry, Kidderminster and Stourbridge. The housing, schools and leisure facilities, details of the local rates and gas and electricity facilities and, of course, the relevant bus services, are given for each location.

Journeys in the Jazz Age

Another 1933 prototype was a new service coach, known as the LRR (Low Rolls-Royce). Like the RR, the esteemed vehicle manufacturer referred to actually had no hand in the new coach. Five more came in 1934, followed by a further 25 in 1935. This was an exotic period for design generally with buses and especially coaches prone to bold liveries. AHA 608 of the 1935 deliveries is in Hereford on 11 August 1939. *John Cull, courtesy The Omnibus Society*

As always, advertising reflected the spirit of the times. These single-fold pocket-size leaflets advertise Anywhere tickets and the Variety Tours book.

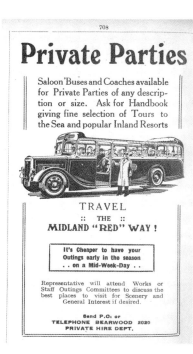

The touring coach fleet was considerably modernised in 1935 with 25 OLR (Open Low Rolls-Royce) models. Like a few other high quality tour operators, Midland Red still considered a bonneted vehicle with driver in the passenger saloon and opening canvas roof was the best specification for a touring coach. The style, however, was on the way out. The OLRs took over what were now called Super-Holiday Tours. In 1932 five tours had been offered, adding the south coast to Devon and Wales. By 1935 this had increased to ten tours, ranging from 2 to 12 days and now including the Scottish Highlands, Yorkshire Dales and the Lake District. There is a London Transport double-decker on a private hire behind AHA 630 so we are not too far from the capital in this view. *J F Higham, courtesy Alan B Cross*

A wooden advertising board promoting the OLR.

Through the 1920s Midland Red published an increasing range of maps, leaflets and guides to promote the regular stage services, 'Anywhere' and excursion tickets, day tours, express services and holiday tours. These came to be offered in a folder called Helps to Happy Holidays which, in the 1930s, were published as one large book. Available from company offices and agencies for 6d (2.5p), Helps to Happy Holidays was a guide to the whole of Great Britain 'for those people to whom holidays by road make a special appeal'.

The 1936 edition has 672 pages, with sections covering Midland Red's Super Holiday Tours; holiday resorts which could be reached by Midland Red or Associated Motorways services; day and half-day tours; and a Gazetteer of the places of interest connected by Midland Red service buses.

"No rules, No rice pudding": There are adverts for leisure attractions, restaurants and boarding houses – over 30 pages are taken up by adverts from Blackpool landladies, and more from other resorts. Lastly, two maps showed the routes of the Super Holiday Tours, to the Scottish Highlands, the Lake District and Wales to Dover and Lands End.

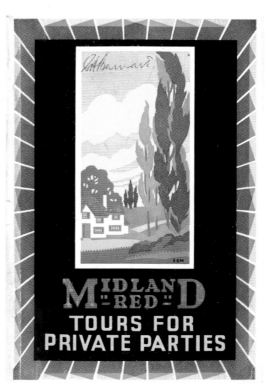

The 1937 Super Holiday Tours guide included a five-day tour to the Yorkshire Dales and Lake District for 7 guineas (£7.35)!

Below
Day and half-day tours were now marketed as 'Mascot Tours'. These were based on the outlines formed by tracing the routes on a map, and naming the tour on the figure suggested by the outline. They included a butterfly tour, a cat tour, a jester tour and many others. The booklet was popular with children, which successfully introduced it into many homes.

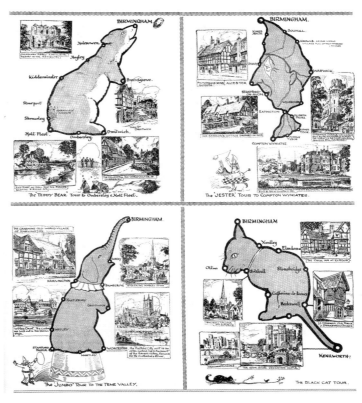

The Streamline Era

The mid-1930s were the height of the streamline era. Although Mr Shire's service buses looked somewhat conservative, the nearside and rear of this 1935 Short-bodied DON, AHA 567, was styling prototype for the 1937 batch of 100 DHA-registered SON buses with English Electric bodies painted in a flamboyant variation of the standard livery. The 1937 SONs would share some of this prototype's styling features with the SLR coaches (see page 50) such as window pillars that widened towards the top, not repeated on subsequent SON deliveries which continued to be received until 1940. It seems probable that this body was merely mocked up rather than physically rebuilt. The windows lack glass rain deflectors and, through them, you can see that the offside pillars are normal. *BMMO, courtesy Kithead Trust*

The comfortable interior of the 1939 SON. *BMMO, courtesy Kithead Trust*

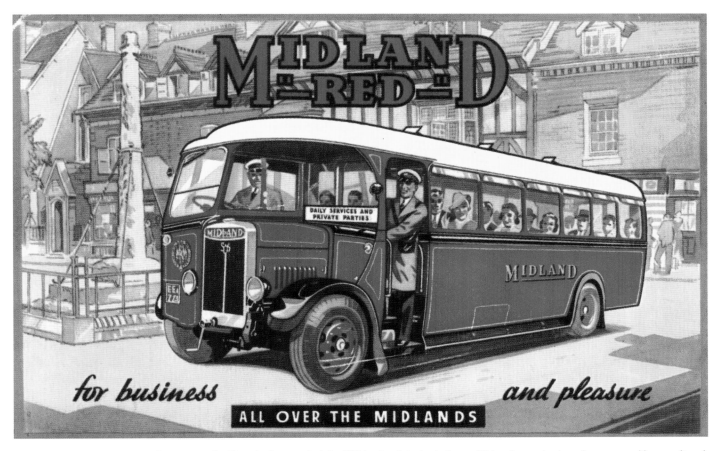

Radiused window corners were by now standard but the front end of the ON family of single-deckers additionally received gentle curves and large radiused corners to the windscreen itself. The front of the roof featured a slight hump, as if a destination blind box was intended but, sadly, the bulkhead stencils and destination boards remained standard, despite roller blinds on the contemporary double-deckers. They also had raised waistrail mouldings which were painted maroon. The garter motif, previously on the rear, was now also carried on the front of the cabs. This postcard shows an EHA-registered SON type delivered in 1938.

Left One of the 1937 DHA buses at work in Worcester with one of the city's attractive shelters prominently carrying the company's name. *R T Wilson/ The Transport Museum, Wythall. Right* The growing number of regulations meant the introduction of fixed stopping places except in deep countryside. Some were compulsory stops for Midland Red drivers while others were by passengers' request. This is an early style of cast iron stop plate without any company identification on it in Shirley. It is being served by a 1936 SON heavily rebuilt post-war and with a non-standard cab. *G H Stone*

The lines of the 50 handsomely rounded SLR class coaches of 1937 were stylish and fashionable. The stepped waistrail had the commendable objective of improving the forward vision of those in the back rows, but perhaps spoiled the otherwise smooth lines. English Electric supplied the 30-seat coachwork to Midland Red design. Smooth running was considered very important for coaches and the full width cabs potentially increased the risk of noise. These, however, originally had SOS petrol engines but would be the last so provided. Leyland E181 7.4 litre diesel engines were fitted after the war for economy, rather a contrast particularly as those units had an intrusive knock.

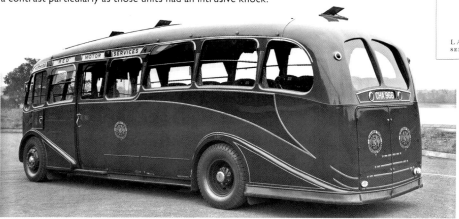

BMMO, courtesy of The Kithead Trust

BMMO, courtesy of The Kithead Trust

The SLRs also worked on Super Holiday Tours which increased in popularity and distance throughout the 1930s. Further developments were planned for the 1940 season but this was not to be. The splendid pre-war view shows CHA 994 on tour in Scotland. *courtesy Kithead Trust*

The Western Highlands
and Royal Deeside
TWELVE DAY COACH CRUISE 1938

MIDLAND
=RED=
Souvenir Itinerary

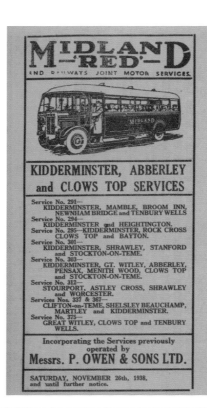

Midland Red had many services into the town so associated with William Shakespeare but did not have the Bard's home to itself. Stratford-upon-Avon Blue Motors was purchased by Midland Red in 1935 and retained as an operating subsidiary for many years. Its retention was surprising enough but, even more extraordinary, Midland Red built buses were not normally supplied to the Stratford subsidiary which standardised initially on second-hand Tilling-Stevens vehicles and, from 1948, on new Leylands. The interesting leaflet (far left) shows what is obviously a SLR posing as a Stratford Blue coach. The reality was rather different. Midland Red took over P. Owen & Sons Ltd of Abberley on 26 November 1938 and passed two of Owen's Maudslay ML3 coaches to Stratford Blue. The Midland Red timetable leaflet includes the services taken over from Owen.

150 FEDDs, delivered in 1938-9, were bodied by Brush to a rather different style. This FHA 200 series FEDD is from a publicity postcard of the time.

The SLRs may have looked modern but one of the outstanding achievements of Mr Shire's team was the production of four prototypes with rear-mounted SOS petrol engines placed into service in 1936-7. The REC classification stood for Rear Engined Coach although actually only CHA 1 was a coach, BHA 1 and CHA 2-3 being service buses. Carlyle Works constructed the bodies which, on the service buses, had the driver sitting ahead of the front axle with the entrance alongside. The SOS petrol engines were positioned transversely at the rear of the chassis frame, behind the rear axle. The three single-deckers were of this appearance and seated 40. Note the garter motif instead of MIDLAND fleetnames. They were not entirely successful and Mr Shire had commenced work on converting the first to underfloor engine when he abruptly retired in 1940. They were fully rebuilt to underfloor in 1942-4, at the start of Mr Sinclair's reign. *BMMO*

The fourth rear-engine prototype was a coach, CHA 1, seating 32 in considerable comfort. This was the first British rear-engined coach, and the technical press praised its riding comfort, passenger accommodation, light steering and easy engine accessibility. Luggage space was provided above the engine and in side lockers. All four RECs were rebuilt as underfloor-engine prototype service buses during World War Two, this coach body being sold. *BMMO, courtesy of Kithead Trust*

The final deliveries of FEDDs and SONs, fifty of each, were received in 1939 and 1940 respectively, around the outbreak of World War Two, and had more rounded rear domes. Above is FHA 236 from the previous delivery of FEDDs, received in 1938-9, which acted as the styling prototype for FHA 836-85, while below is GHA325, a Brush bodied SON of 1940. The FEDDs received the interesting treatment to the silver-painted roof shown but the fifty SONs were given red roofs as shown below, which distinguished them from previous models and provided a styling link to the S-series single-deckers after the war. This distinction disappeared when buses received khaki brown roofs during World War Two, to reduce their visibility to enemy aircraft, but reappeared upon the return of peace. *BMMO, courtesy of Kithead Trust*

The 25 ONC (ON Coach) vehicles of 1939 were the first coaches with diesel engines. Their Duple 30-seat bodies introduced the simple but effective livery of red below the waistrail and black above that became standard for coaches, including the SLRs, after World War Two.
The war meant serious cuts in services with railways covering the long-distance demands and all coach tours ceased at the end of the 1939 season. The oldest (RR and SRR) coaches were loaned out while the middle-aged LRR service coaches and OLR touring vehicles were converted to buses. The OLRs were extensively rebuilt from normal to forward control to allow 34 seats, a useful increase of five. This left only the 75 SLR and ONC types for coach duties when peace returned in 1945. The ONCs were still in general use until 1958-60 with FHA 418 retained until 1963 because the sliding roof was useful for special occasions such as victorious football teams!

FHA 425 was numerically the last of the ONCs. It carried experimental features in its early years, then being classified LON (Luxury ON) and was the vehicle used to transport the Directors. Those glamorous duties long since handed on to a later generation, FHA 425 is seen in St James Street, Leicester, where a spare coach or two was often parked in case extras were required for excursions departing from Humberstone Gate.
Ken Jubb

Route maps showing
DON HA 9485 and
FEDD HA 9429.

The date is uncertain for
this cautionary poster
but it would have been
highly relevant during
World War Two.

The Sinclair Years

DONALD MCINTYRE SINCLAIR CBE

Donald Sinclair was born and raised in Glasgow. He served an apprenticeship with Albion Motors, was involved in bus operation in Perthshire and became a regional transport engineer at BP. In 1931 he was appointed assistant to Gordon Hayter, the highly innovative Chief Engineer of Northern General, which operated a large number of Midland Red-built SOS buses. He was therefore familiar with their capabilities, but was equally radical in exploring new engine positions to maximise the seating capacity of single-deckers.

In 1940 Sinclair was appointed Chief Engineer of Midland Red on the retirement of L G Wyndham Shire and, on the sudden death of O C Power in October 1943, he became General Manager and Chief Engineer. He disliked the SOS branding, which he removed from the vehicles, and post-war Midland Red vehicles would be badged BMMO, the company's initials.

Mr Shire's designs had been generally conservative in appearance but, under Sinclair, the Company's products would prove both innovative and stylish. He rebuilt the four rear-engined REC vehicles with underfloor engines, which he believed to be the way forward. His building in quantity of underfloor engined single-deckers and coaches in the late 1940s was several years ahead of the rest of the industry.

In 1945, he produced the post-war double decker prototype, HHA1. The rear entrance followed experience with the wartime utility buses, but also the change to rear entrance double-deckers at Northern General in 1939.

DMS, as he became known, not only continued to guide Midland Red's engineering developments but also ably grasped the demanding role of operating the largest bus company in England during a period of considerable expansion and then contraction. Midland Red, having developed and operated in separate engineering and traffic halves before World War Two, needed a quite exceptional person to streamline it into one organisation (well, almost!). He reorganised his management team in 1946, appointing S C Vince to the role of Chief Engineer.

In 1948 Sinclair travelled to the USA to study the bus industry there, visiting manufacturers and operators. He was impressed by the Greyhound coach operation, which would have influenced his development of motorway express services ten years later. A more immediate result was the rebuilding of an S9 into 'the American S9', looking very like US buses of the time.

Sinclair was awarded the CBE in 1950, and was President of the Omnibus Society in 1953. He continued to lead bus development forward with lighter, integral, vehicles using fibreglass, rubber suspension and disc brakes. This culminated in the CM5T, and later CM6T, motorway coaches, and the D9 and D10 double deckers. He also campaigned for longer vehicles for the motorway service, and pushed forward with a building programme for garages, Central Works and the Birmingham bus station. He insisted that Midland Red's engineering achievements were the result of teamwork, not of one person, and that credit should go to all parts of the Engineering Department aided by suggestions from the Traffic Department.

Donald Sinclair was a family man, but was considered dour and remote by many of those who worked for him. He retired in 1966.

The production of buses, including Midland Red's own vehicles, ceased at the start of the War. In addition to the khaki roofs, another step to make buses less visible to enemy aircraft was the masking of exterior and interior lights, making life especially hard for night drivers and conductors and explaining the white paint edging the vehicles. The Ministry of Supply eventually permitted the limited production of buses. Midland Red's completely SOS fleet was joined between 1942 and 1945 by a mixed selection of double-deckers built by Leyland, AEC, Guy and Daimler. The six 1942 Brush-bodied AEC Regents were designed to the order of Coventry Corporation but, despite the massive blitz damage in that city, allocated to Midland Red. GHA 797 demonstrates the wartime khaki roof, white lining and masked headlights.
The Omnibus Society

Midland Red style was largely suspended for the duration of World War Two. The Ministry of War Transport distributed austerity standard buses with wooden slatted seats to operators, Midland Red receiving a considerable number of Guy Arabs and Daimlers. The Guys were allocated to Sutton Coldfield and Leicester. 2506, with Weymann body, is the star of this August 1950 scene, illustrating the dubious concrete splendour of Leicester's St Margaret's bus station. The date is 5 August 1950 and the Guy would have received upholstered seats by this time. *Roy Marshall*

1936 SOS FEDD BHA 344 in wartime garb with masked headlights and Metro-Cammell 56-seat body looking neglected. Many staff had gone to war so engineering attention had to concentrate on safety critical items. This Birmingham loading point is interesting, being at the western end of Great Charles Street, not usually associated with Midland Red buses. As a fuel saving measure from 1 December 1941, the terminal point of all Hagley Road services after 4pm on Mondays to Fridays and 12 noon on Saturdays was moved from Station Street to here, approached via Edmund Street and Congreve Street – these sections of road no longer exist. The usual Station Street arrangements were resumed from 25 June 1945. The entrance to an air raid shelter is on the right. Birmingham City Transport for many years occupied the offices in Congreve Street, visible beyond the Austin car.
The Omnibus Society

The Daimler CWA6 austerity buses were allocated to Birmingham's Digbeth garage, later becoming associated with Sheepcote Street garage after that opened. The Daimlers' preselector gearboxes were useful in the city's traffic but, here, Brush-bodied 2548 has escaped on one of Digbeth's longer services. It is seen in the Red Lion bus station, Stratford-upon-Avon, southern terminus of the 150 from Birmingham. *J F Higham/ courtesy Alan B Cross*

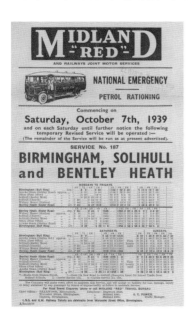

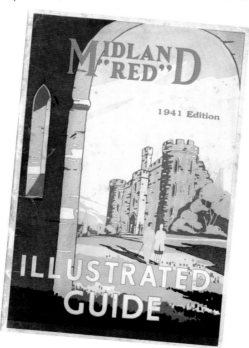

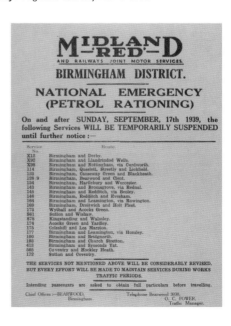

Both Mr Shire, before his retirement, and Mr Sinclair were interested in moving the engine under the floor to provide more passenger-carrying space. These thoughts did not extend, for the time being, to double-deckers because of the effect on overall height. Instead Mr Sinclair modernised their appearance dramatically by concealing the radiator. The first experiment, completed in 1942, involved this 1938 FEDD, the rebuilding also including the front of the upper deck with a clear hint of styling to come. *BMMO, courtesy of Kithead Trust*

All the Brush bodies on FEDD chassis needed extensive rebuilding in 1949-51, nearly all being attended to by Aero & Engineering (Merseyside) Ltd, Hooton. The rubber mounted flush glazing with sliding vents was part of the standard rebuild package but EHA 299 lost its concealed radiator too. Its front upper deck windows remained distinctive, however. It is seen about to take up a duty from Bearwood garage. *G H Stone*

The prototype post-war double-decker entered service in 1945, classified D1, carrying the registration HHA 1 and fleet number 2541. Metro-Cammell had not yet resumed body production so Weymann, its partner, built the sleek all-metal body. The wartime deliveries had confirmed the superiority of the rear entrance for rapid loading of double-deck buses. The D1 also featured only four, longer, window bays on the lower deck, like the London RT, plus much improved destination blind arrangements.
The Omnibus Society

The "wheel" symbol first appeared on the new Staff Information Bulletin in September 1946, and the February 1947 issue reported that it had been adopted by the Company for publicity purposes.

Midland Red continued during World War Two to work on prototypes for post-war production. Mr Sinclair was convinced that the underfloor engine was the future for single-deckers and his team rebuilt the four pre-war rear-engine vehicles to this layout. The bodies were swapped around with the solitary coach body being sold and a new service bus body built for the final prototype at Carlyle Road Works. A new type numbering system was introduced in 1945, S, D and C for single-decker, double-decker buses, and coaches. The four underfloor engine prototypes became the S1 to S4 models – CHA 2 here was the S3. *BMMO, courtesy of Kithead Trust*

CHA 3 received the new body, built in 1944, to become the S4. The company's Private Identification Numbers were adopted as fleet numbers in that year, this bus coincidentally being number 1944. It spent most of its S4 career working from Stourbridge garage but is seen here on the large yard in front of Midland Red's Birmingham Digbeth garage and coach station, available to the company until the road was widened to dual carriageway. *G H Stone*

An entirely new S5 prototype, registered HHA 222, was completed in 1946. This introduced chassisless construction and, contrary to previous belief, was built entirely at Carlyle Works and not bodied by Metro-Cammell, although the latter assisted the project. Between the end of 1946 and mid-1951, 500 buses and 57 coaches with underfloor engines were placed into service, before the big manufacturers caught up. *Metro-Cammell*

With the need for quick deliveries, the complications of chassisless construction were shelved for the time being. The early post-war single-deck buses and coaches were thus body on chassis, the favoured coachbuilders being Metro-Cammell and Brush, constructing to Midland Red's designs. The S6 model adopted the longer windows introduced on the D1 and sliding ventilators became standard. The streamlined appearance of the post-war fleet was followed through with livery simplifications, notably the red roofs. The D1's destination layout was also adopted with its three-track number blind, the first track also including the local service prefix letters. The separate destination (upper) and via (lower) blinds were known internally as 'A' and 'B' blinds. After a short while, blinds very usefully featured the garage code to the extreme left of the display. The body of 27 ft 6 ins length accommodated 40 seats. There was a hinged door manually operated by the conductor provided at the saloon entrance, level with the rear of the driver's cab. This arrangement looks archaic now power doors are universal but the S6, in its time, was the trendsetter for the industry. *Roy Marshall*

Cab access was by a separate, hinged, door on the offside. The shape of the sliding window in the cab door is a work of art. This little window would be much used as hand signals were essential, the driver did not have any mechanical or electrical means of indicating his intentions. *Metro-Cammell*

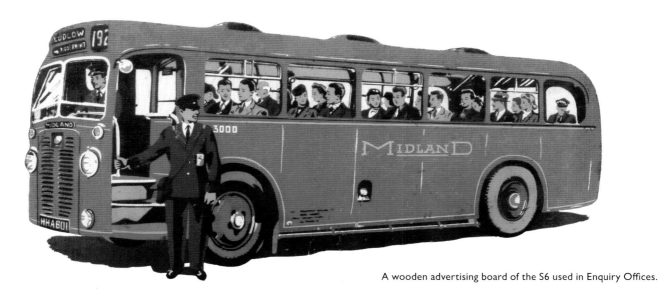

A wooden advertising board of the S6 used in Enquiry Offices.

With BMMO capacity fully occupied building revolutionary single-deckers, the first 100 post-war double-deckers, delivered between 1948 and 1950, were based on AEC Regent II chassis and classified AD2. The bodies closely resembled the D1 prototype, the contract being split equally between Brush (including 3112 here) and Metro-Cammell. BMMO's own D5 model began to enter service in 1949. These buses all shared a rather worried look which was accentuated when they were fitted with ventilators in the front dome. *Brush*

The 50 Brush AD2s were all received in 1948 but Metro-Cammell's contribution of 50 bodies was seriously delayed. This bus was the only one received in 1949, the rest not being delivered until 1950. An increased number of sliding ventilators was standard by this time. *Metro-Cammell*

Interior of AD2 3160.
Metro-Cammell

Faced with slow supply of double-deck buses, Midland Red took the opportunity in 1949 to buy 20 Guy Arab III vehicles, available with quick delivery. The bodies were also built by Guy, on Park Royal frames, paying no regard to BMMO views on styling. Midland Red classified them GD6; it will be noticed from these and the AD2s that non-BMMO types were prefixed with the first letter of the manufacturer. The buses, numbered 3557-76, were allocated to Dudley garage where their large Meadows 6DC 10.35 litre engines made short work of the many hills in the district. Unfortunately the engines were thirsty and awkward to maintain in the Guy Arab, although no doubt good in other applications. After trying a GD6 with a Gardner 5LW, all twenty were fitted with BMMO 8 litre engines in 1952. No 3575 is seen in Chamberlain Place, Birmingham. *Roy Marshall*

Several hundred similar but wider buses followed the S6, the type numbers extending upwards to S12. The permitted maximum length for single-deck buses was increased from 27 feet 6 inches to 30 feet from 1 June 1950. Double-deckers could be 27 feet, an increase of one foot, from the same date – 30 feet double-deckers had to wait until 1 July 1956. The S12s took advantage of the new dimension, being 29 ft 3 in long, giving space for 44 seats. All the earlier post-war single-deckers were extended to the same length and upseated to 44 between 1951 and 1953. Lengthened S10 3606, with Brush body, loads at Pool Meadow, Coventry, in September 1955, and still carries the pre-spray paint livery and lining out. *Bruce Jenkins*

A new style bus stop plate with the company's post-war 'wheel' symbol logo became very familiar after World War Two. Normally rectangular, this version was used in Birmingham to fit the round stops provided by the city's transport department. The bus is a S12 model and the location Rednal, home of a massive tramcar terminus, much enjoyed by Brummies savouring the Lickey Hills on fine bank holidays in the first half of the twentieth century. *Michael Rooum*

Far left Important bus stops had additional information on the plate, in this instance at Wednesbury combined with a pre-war timetable case. Later cases would also have the wheel symbol. The bus stop plate is not as old as one might think as the 862 and 867 were created in a December 1966 service revision. *Ken Jubb*

Left This display flies the company flag in distant Melton Mowbray bus station. Barton buses are a delicious temptation in the background. *Ken Jubb*

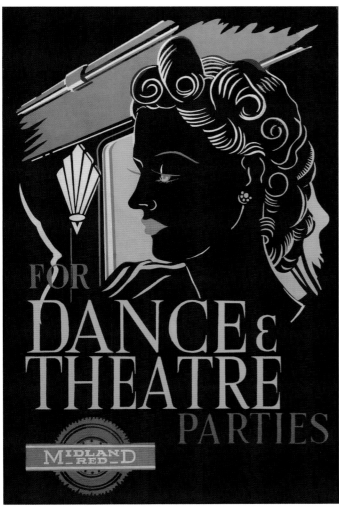

SYMONDS YAT. SERVICE 413 FROM BIRMINGHAM & WORCESTER (SUMMER ONLY) SUNDAYS

A fascinating beauty spot, with its wooded hills and steep cliffs reaching down to the waters edge. An ideal place for an outing.

DAILY TOURS DURING THE SEASON FROM CHIEF MIDLAND RED CENTRES.

This is how the OLR-class normal control char-a-bancs, new in 1935, looked after wartime rebuilding to fully enclosed forward control service buses. Also worth a look in this view of Dudley Street, Birmingham, is the signwriting for the company's parcels office. *G H Stone*

Pre-war buses largely reverted to their old liveries, for the time being at least, apart from the loss of the maroon (ON family single-deckers) or cream (double-deckers) relief bands. The old fleetnames continued too although the new post-war style was applied to many buses that had extensive body rebuilding and, eventually, to the entire fleet, including surviving unrebuilt pre-war buses. This interesting vehicle was built in 1934 as a petrol-engined ON with body by Short Bros. It was converted to diesel with one of the company's 8 litre units in 1938 and reclassified CON (Converted ON). One of a small number of buses rebuilt at Carlyle Works with metal sides after the Second World War, it is bearing the post-war fleetname while loading in Station Street, Birmingham, alongside a shelter carrying the earlier style. *N S Stone*

Not all the ON family single-deckers received major body rebuilds. Those unrebuilt had shorter lives and some formed the base for auxiliary vehicles. One 1935 example that had remained a true ON with SOS petrol engine, AHA 519, was converted in 1952 to a mobile publicity vehicle, attending major public events to publicise the company's activities. In 1955 the body was transferred to AHA 527, a member of the CON class, another ON converted to diesel in 1938. AHA 527 was sold for scrap in May 1964.
R Mallabon/ The Transport Museum, Wythall

Leicester-based 1938 FEDD 2120, with Brush body rebuilt at Hooton in 1951, loads at one of the concrete shelters designed by the company. The raised MIDLAND legend was cast into the concrete and painted red.
Michael Rooum

Most of the wartime buses were, of necessity, built to austere specification. Nearly all had very severe lines, including unradiused rear domes, and most deteriorated quickly due to the unseasoned timber used for the body frames. It was necessary to rebuild those bodies fairly early in life so Midland Red took the opportunity to soften their appearance in a number of ways. Rounded rear domes and radiused glazing were improvements made by many operators but Midland Red went a step further by building up the front wings, as an easier option to concealing the radiators. One Guy and one Daimler had their bodies rebuilt by Carlyle as styling prototypes as early as 1949; Brush and Willowbrook did the work on most of the remainder in 1950-1. This is 2546, the 1945 Daimler CWA6 with Brush body rebuilt by Carlyle. Despite this work, Midland Red sold off these non-standard buses at around eleven years of age although most found new owners. *BMMO, courtesy Kithead Trust*

The 1951 route map included this drawing of the D1 updated with a D5 registration number. Donald Sinclair introduced the phrase 'The Friendly Midland Red' in 1949 and it continued in use until the late 1960s.

Chief Offices:
BEARWOOD, BIRMINGHAM
Telephone: BEARWOOD 3030

D.M.SINCLAIR C.B.E.,M.Inst.T.,M.I.Mech.E., GENERAL MANAGER

The friendly Midland Red
FREE ENTERPRISE AT YOUR SERVICE

MIDLAND RED

ROUTE MAP
WITH
NOTES ON PLACES
OF INTEREST

Mr Sinclair was determined to improve BMMO buses further. He undertook a long tour of North America in 1948 and set up Bus Design Committees the next year. 1945 D1 post-war prototype 2541 became the first bus with power operated platform doors when they were fitted in 1949. More radical was bus 3441, often called the American S9, entering service in March 1950 with this BMMO built front end, becoming the first single-decker with power operated platform doors. Cab access was via the saloon instead of a separate door on the offside and the cab itself was not partitioned from the passenger accommodation. The generous brightwork was a feature of Midland Red prototypes around this time.
BMMO, courtesy Kithead Trust

The integral concept had been put on ice after the S5 but the company's aim to produce a lightweight, chassisless design reappeared with the solitary LA (Light Alloy), constructed in 1951. This bus, fleet number 3977, was only in stock for ten years and then scrapped but it led directly to the chassisless S14 and all other subsequent BMMO designs, including the D9 and D10 double-deckers. This delightful view of 3977 and an obviously captivating young lady in Navigation Street, Birmingham also shows a nicely signwritten temporary stop, arguably only let down by being jammed into an old wheel – a common practice in the industry! *Roy Marshall*

Pursuing the Romantic Dream

Holiday Tours recommenced in the late 1940s and were now called Coach Cruises. The 1949 brochure was very simple, illustrated only by a line drawing on the cover. It proudly announced that 'a fleet of new coaches, built to the traditional Midland Red standards of comfort and dependability' would be operated. There were 11 different cruises, varying from 5 to 14 days, to Devon, Cornwall, the South Coast and Isle of Wight, Scotland, Yorkshire Dales and English Lakes. Patrons were not required to surrender their ration books, still in use from World War Two, but were to bring their own soap and towels. Each coach had a driver and a courier, and some Cruises also operated from Leicester.

The 1950 programme had a black and white picture of a C1 on the cover, but announced the C2s, new coaches that 'will provide extremely comfortable seating for 26 passengers'. There would be no conductor, and the Driver/Courier ("the skipper") would be 'so positioned inside the vehicle as to be in constant contact with his passengers.' Later brochures showed the C2 and C4 coaches, and destinations now included Ireland.

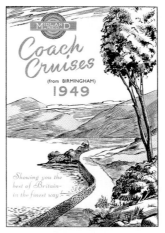

8 feet wide buses had been permitted from 1 July 1946 but their routes needed special dispensation for some years. Because they could be required to go almost anywhere, the first post-war coaches were thus built to the earlier width of 7 feet 6 inches. Chassis were based on the underfloor-engine service buses, comprising 45 C1 models, delivered in 1948-9 with 30-seat bodies, followed by the dozen C2 touring coaches in 1950, all 57 being bodied by Duple. As the driver sitting with his passengers remained such a desirable feature of tour coaches, the partition around him was dispensed with on the C2.
The C1s had sliding doors while those on the C2s were hinged. An at-a-glance recognition point was that both front screens were recessed on the C2. Monograms continued to be favoured for coaches in lieu of fleet names but the post-war types received a simplified style. C2 3349 passes through a busy Matlock Bath. *The Transport Museum, Wythall*

The 1950 brochure for coach cruises in Britain gave options for holidays of between 4 and 13 days, with prices inclusive of accommodation and meals.

In 1953, the Publicity Department provided the front cover photograph for a brochure on Seeing Britain by Road published by the British Travel and Holidays Association. This was distributed worldwide to encourage tourism by coach, car, motorcycle and bicycle in Coronation Year. The picture shoot took place in Chaddesley Corbett, Worcestershire, with C1 coach 3303, and Eunice Hough of the Publicity Department and Alan Kelsall of the Tours Department posing with their bicycles. The hikers just happened to be passing, and were 'recruited' for the picture! The pictures were used in Midland Red publicity throughout the 'fifties and into the 'sixties.

TINTERN ABBEY   Monmouthshire

One of many lovely places
visited by our

DAY & HALF DAY TOURS

* See weekly Folders and Press announcements

One of a series of posters advertising day tours and excursions by coach. Day Tours were increasingly popular through the 1950s, to beauty spots in and around the Midlands. The poster for Coach Cruises (right) was for the advertising panel in the lower saloon of double-deckers, on the rear of the staircase.

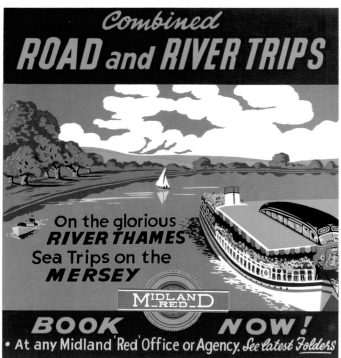

1950s posters promoting trips and cruises.

The C2 coaches did not have roof lights, but this poster gives a foretaste of the coming C4s.

The Newbury A34 bypass was a controversial construction but the previous congestion was a daunting prospect, particularly at holiday times. This comfort break at Newbury was no doubt very welcome for the passengers aboard C1 3343 in August 1962. *F W York/ The Transport Museum, Wythall*

Carlyle Works built the body for the first C4 cruise coach, 4242, in 1953. This acted as style prototype for the 63 C3 service coaches, 4179-4241 bodied by Willowbrook, and the remaining 11 C4s that followed. C4s 4243-53 were bodied by Alexander, then little known in England and willing to build a small number of bodies to BMMO's design. The C4s could be recognised at a glance by their roof windows and some had their grilles modified as shown here on 4253 at Aldershot. *John May*

Private Hire

FOR
PRIVATE
PARTIES

MIDLAND RED

BIRMINGHAM AREA
INCLUDING BLACK COUNTRY, BROMSGROVE AND REDDITCH

Luxury Coaches, specially designed for long distance touring and built to the traditional Midland 'Red' standards of comfort and dependability, will be employed on all Cruises. Each coach will be in the charge of an experienced Driver/Courier.

The illustrations show the two types of coaches—the 36 seater (below) used for ALL Cruises with the exception of R, X, SPC/3 and SPC/4, which will be operated with the 30 seater type as top illustration.

Anyone thinking C3 4193 is somewhere in the outer suburbs of Birmingham's former tramway system would be somewhat wide of the mark – it is actually in Colwyn Bay in July 1956. *The Transport Museum, Wythall*

C4 vehicles operated most coach cruises in the later 1950s. Most C2s were upseated for normal express and excursion work but a few were retained as tour coaches over roads needing smaller vehicles. The company made many in-house promotional films during this time with music by the company's own orchestra and singers. Traffic Manager Richard Brandon took a very close interest, including filming Midland Red coaches encountered during his own holidays and providing some of the films' commentaries.

1950s posters for tours and private hire by C3 and C4 coach. The Talyllyn Railway was a popular destination. The Cruise brochure again extols 'olde England'.

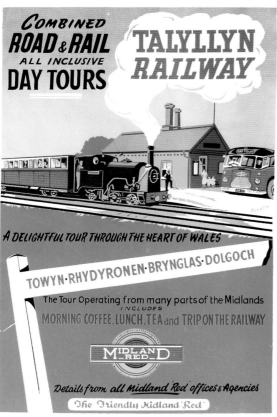

At the Peak

The 1952 BMMO AGM report stated that the 1951 vehicle production programme had been affected by the rearmament programme, although it was not made clear whether this was a labour or materials shortage. This was the time of the Korean War, for which armaments would be needed. Presumably Carlyle Works was suffering from people leaving for better pay at BSA or the like so 100 Leyland double-deck buses were ordered to compensate for the shortfall, The Directors also announced at the 1952 AGM that 'In addition, during the five-year period 1953-58, the construction of a further 718 vehicles has been authorised, 373 of which will be double deck, 270 single deck, and 75 will be coaches. The effect of this programme will be that, when completed, your Company will have in service the maximum number of double deck vehicles which road obstructions and the like make it possible to operate; the pre-war fleet will have been replaced; and such expansion as at present can be foreseen will have been provided for. It will also ensure that the whole of your Company's fleet will be of maximum seating capacity permitted by the Regulations'. In the event, the 373 double-deckers only numbered 350, forming the new D7 class.

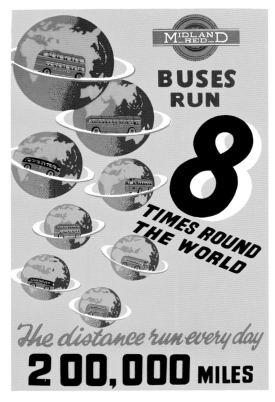

These 1950s posters showed Midland Red's justifiable pride in its reputation and achievements. Passenger numbers reached 484 million, and mileage 79 million, in 1956. The fleet peaked at 1,910 buses and coaches in 1954 though the slight reduction in the following years was through the use of larger vehicles. The poster shows a D5B type, the first production series of buses with platform doors, a total of 100 being built with bodies by Brush between 1950 and 1952.

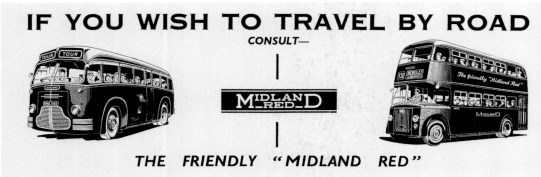

An advertisement in a local road map using the last coach and double-deck bus line drawings of this style: including the LD8. There is also a drawing of the S13 single-decker, but later vehicles were photographed or drawn in an entirely different way.

The company had been specifying passenger heaters for some time but the platform doors meant that riders could enjoy the full benefit. The doors were power operated by the driver, with emergency buttons on the platform available to the conductor. It looks a useful day for the new features as D5B 3859 works a Shrewsbury town service. *Michael Rooum*

Midland Red's first production series of single-deck buses with power doors were the S13s. These were built to the new length of 30 feet and capable of seating 44. Nearly all, however, were finished as dual-purpose buses with superior seating for 40. They were used on the company's longer stage carriage services but also adequate to assist the coach fleet at times of pressure. Brush-bodied 3885 is loading at Victoria Coach Station, London, around the time of the Coronation of Queen Elizabeth II in June 1953, explaining the ER and flags above the destination box. *The Transport Museum, Wythall collection*

D5 3553 was fitted with this grille with vertical slots that had more than a passing resemblance to Birmingham City Transport's design. A simplified version was evolved for the forthcoming D7, and the Leyland-built LD8 that endeavoured to resemble the D7. *Gordon Davies*

The 100 Leylands were classified LD8. D5B 3872 was sent to Leyland in early 1952 as an example of the current Midland Red standard. Leyland exhibited the first LD8, 3978, at the 1952 Commercial Motor Show while the others arrived in early 1953. Leyland developed a full-width bonnet comparable to the Midland Red design but, due to the raked design of the standard Leyland body, it was not flush with the front of the bus. Interest at the 1952 Show in the new front led to it being offered as an option by Leyland, retaining the space at the top of the grille for the BMMO symbol! It became widely used throughout the UK and on export Titans too so Midland Red style became familiar on the streets of Madrid, for example. Leyland ceased building its excellent bus bodies in 1954 so the LD8s were the only examples combining Leyland bodies and BMMO bonnets, though some Edinburgh Leyland-bodied Titans were later fitted with them. While Show vehicle 3978 had gold lining, yellow was now standard. The 1685 Group, based at Wythall, completed in 2010 restoration of the sole survivor, 4031, to original condition. *Malcolm Keeley*

ARLEY-ON-SEVERN FROM KIDDERMINSTER. SERVICE NO. 298.
Visit this delightful village with its picturesque cottages, set amidst beautiful woods on the Severn. There are dozens of charming walks. A fine centre for boating, fishing and camping, an ideal spot for a day's outing.

MIDLAND RED D

SEE THE COUNTRYSIDE FROM THE BUS WINDOW

RIVER TEME and BRIDGE *TENBURY WELLS*
A pretty market town bordering Shropshire and Herefordshire, lying in a fertile Valley. A good centre for anglers, hikers and picnic parties.

ALWAYS *TRAVEL*

MIDLAND RED D

SEE THE COUNTRYSIDE FROM THE BUS WINDOW

A series of 1950s posters showed views of the Midlands from the bus window.

STONELEIGH ABBEY *FROM COVENTRY & LEAMINGTON. SERVICE NOS. 567,587,588.*
Founded in the reign of Henry II. The buildings shown here, date from 1720-1726. Contains rare paintings & furnishings, the finest in the country. Situated in a lovely stretch of parkland near the Avon.

VISITED BY OUR DAY & HALF DAY TOURS

MIDLAND RED D

SEE THE COUNTRYSIDE FROM THE BUS WINDOW

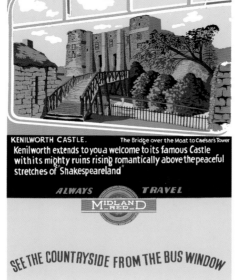

KENILWORTH CASTLE. The Bridge over the Moat to Caesar's Tower
Kenilworth extends to you a welcome to its famous Castle with its mighty ruins rising romantically above the peaceful stretches of "Shakespeareland"

ALWAYS *TRAVEL*

MIDLAND RED D

SEE THE COUNTRYSIDE FROM THE BUS WINDOW

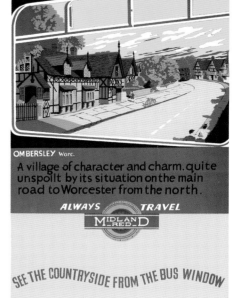

OMBERSLEY Worc.
A village of character and charm, quite unspoilt by its situation on the main road to Worcester from the north.

ALWAYS *TRAVEL*

MIDLAND RED D

SEE THE COUNTRYSIDE FROM THE BUS WINDOW

The Economies Begin

The paint spray booth was one of the proudest features of the new Central Works but it encouraged the introduction of an unrelieved red livery across the fleet from mid-1955. Pre-war vehicles retained black wings on repaints until 1957 but red has finally enveloped the rebuilt Brush body of 1938 FEDD 2224 seen in Newark Street, Leicester, in June 1958. *Bruce Jenkins*

350 D7s entered service between 1953 and 1957. Their Metro-Cammell bodies were modern in appearance but, to be truthful, were rather cheap and nasty. Their light weight achieved necessary fuel savings and meant that they were eager workhorses. Metro-Cammell continued to deliver D7s in traditional livery until April 1956 when all-over red took over, the earlier ones receiving it on repaint. No 4389 loads in Nuneaton bus station. *John May*

The interiors of the D7s were bright but plain. This is the lower saloon of 4086. *Metro-Cammell*

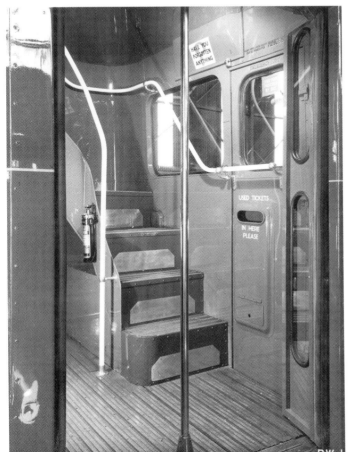

The platform of D7 4086 complete with the fondly remembered 'Have you forgotten anything?' notice. *Metro-Cammell*

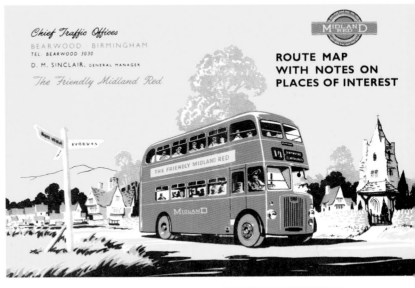

The final stage of Carlyle Works' reconstruction was the new Body Shop that allowed the large-scale production of bodies, instead of using outside coachbuilders working to the company's designs. The first bulk production of BMMO bodies was the lightweight 'chassisless' S14 class which entered service from 1955. The neat looking S14 was the culmination of development work with earlier chassisless experimental vehicles but, with single rear wheels as part of the weight savings, not particularly comfortable over a distance. They were in the vanguard of the move towards buses without conductors. S14 4709 awaits its next work at Evesham. *Ken Jubb*

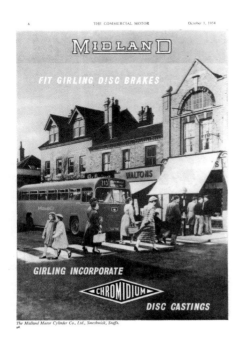

While Midland Red vehicles were not for sale on the open market, manufacturers were eager to quote the company's use of their products. The 1954 Commercial Motor Show included several Midland Red items on the suppliers' stands. Metalastik exhibited a model of the S14 underframe to demonstrate their rubber suspension. Girling showed a disc brake system developed jointly with Midland Red, Metal Sections of Oldbury had an S14 underframe as their main exhibit, and Docker Brothers of Birmingham showed an example of plastic panelling pioneered by Midland Red.

An Austin 25 cwt van (familiarly known as the Three-way) new in 1950 and surprisingly carrying the pre-war style of fleetname. *BMMO, courtesy Kithead Trust*

The Publicity Department's new Morris Minor van in March 1956. *BMMO, courtesy Kithead Trust*

One of many Morris-Commercial lorries in the service vehicle fleet, typically used to take items for repair at Central Works and return with overhauled or new parts. Rugby's example is seen outside its home garage. Above its bonnet can be seen chalked or partly painted advertisement boards promoting Midland Red excursions. *Ken Jubb*

Midland Red had a fleet of dual-purpose buses, i.e. single-deckers with better quality seating able to assist the coach fleet at busy times and used at other times on longer stage carriage services. These received the red and black coach livery from 1956. At the time this involved the S13 class which retained bus fleetnames. This is 3943 at Myton Road garage, Leamington. *Ken Jubb*

In 1956, Marilyn Monroe starred in the movie 'Bus Stop', which was based in the USA. Ever ready to take advantage of an opportunity, Midland Red arranged to place recruitment publicity in cinemas showing the film. Here Marilyn poses with an S15, quite a contrast to the silver-sided long-distance American coach in the film!

The ODD COLUMN

"BUS STOP"

Day Anywhere tickets were very popular on the long stage carriage routes served by the fifty S15 buses, 4601-50, new in 1957 and wearing the red and black livery introduced on S13s the previous year. These seated 40 in greater comfort than the 44 of the equivalent S14. No sign of Marilyn alongside 4643 at Hereford, waiting for departure time on the infrequent 409 service to Birmingham.
R Mallabon/ The Transport Museum, Wythall

SOME of our readers will have seen, or will be seeing within the next few weeks, the new film featuring Marilyn Monroe entitled "Bus Stop." The film was shown at the Futurist Theatre in Birmingham before Christmas, and amongst other theatres where it has been or will be seen in the early future are: The "Clifton" at Wolverhampton, The "Empire" at Walsall, The "Essoldo" at Leicester, and The "Essoldo" at Loughborough.

With the co-operation of the 20th-Century-Fox-Film organisation, a special "dioramic" publicity-display has been (or will be) on show in the foyers of the cinemas at which the film is appearing, inviting patrons interested in "a good regular job" to join the Midland 'Red' as Driver, Conductor or Conductress. The display includes a model Midland 'Red' bus and bus stop sign, and the entire display is about 6ft. high and 5ft. wide. A photograph of the display is reproduced above.

This is a valuable piece of recruiting publicity for the Company —and no doubt for the film as well—and we are hoping that it will produce good results of mutual advantage to the cinemas concerned and to our Staff Department.

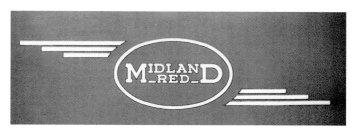

The early post-war fleet numbers were yellow, shaded black. It was not until early 1956 that unshaded numerals were introduced to match the post-war fleetname and the earlier style would still be seen for a number of years. Two ONCs, 2282 and 2289, demonstrate the styles. Of particular interest here are the other fleet numbers, MR5 and MR9. Some ONC coaches were surplus to Midland Red requirements by the time of these 1959 photographs and Black & White Motorways hired ten, giving them numbers MR1 to 10. *Ken Jubb*

The BMMO monogram familiarly used on the traditional coaches. Interestingly, the C2, C3 and C4 vehicles had the three flashes each side seen here but the C1 coaches did not. *Ken Jubb*

The modernised version of the winged logo, with Midland Red rather than BMMO – meaningless to many – applied to the sides of the S15 dual-purpose vehicles, built in 1957 and 1962, instead of the large fleetname. It was also used on the C5 family of vehicles. *Ken Jubb*

The CM5T received the ultimate accolade of being illustrated in the 'Eagle' comic and the interest of many Midland Red enthusiasts dates from this exciting time. The company encouraged this interest by issuing photographs of the latest buses and the much-loved and regularly updated pink fleet list book, all free. The small army of enthusiasts were particular users of the Day Anywhere all-day rides tickets reintroduced in 1958. Separate leaflets were issued suggesting Day Anywhere trips from towns and cities around the Midlands. With the Gazetteer booklet produced each year, these were the successors to the Variety Tours booklets of the 1930s.

Into the Motorway Age on Day One

Midland Red's most famous design was the C5 which entered production in 1959. Its main claim to fame was the turbocharged CM5T variant that, on 2 November 1959, introduced motorway express services to Britain, cruising at 80 mph, giving the company immense operational and technical prestige. The seating capacity was reduced from 37 to 34 as the "T" indicated that the vehicle was fitted with a toilet compartment, previously a rare feature on British coaches as comfort breaks were usual. In addition to the turbocharged engine, the CM5T had a different rear axle ratio and larger front tyres. Here are genuinely excited passengers and possibly apprehensive drivers for the first service journey of the motorway coach age, being worked by nos 4804 and 4809. *The Transport Museum, Wythall collection*

A rather delightful, albeit antiquated, feature was the wooden routeboard on each side above the windows. Here, in the earliest motorway days, CM5T 4801 receives a tyre check at London Victoria Coach Station. It has to be remembered that, for the first time, British coaches were being asked to operate at sustained speeds of 80 mph and unofficially more! Not long before, the maximum permitted speed had been 30 mph although this was often exceeded. The front panel carries a cast handwritten Midland Red fleetname that was later used more widely on the company's coaches and dual-purpose vehicles. *Ken Jubb*

DAY and MIDLAND RED HALF DAY
COACH Tours
COUNTRY and SEASIDE
STATELY HOMES
PLEASURE GROUNDS
RACE MEETINGS

"Make your HOME—
Your holiday centre."

FULL DETAILS AVAILABLE FROM :-
MIDLAND RED OFFICES throughout the Midlands

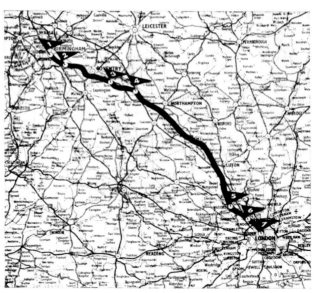

Midland Red tackles Britain's toughest course
(And provides a 6,000,000 mile testimonial for Shell Rotella T oil)

1 Leave Birmingham. Crawl for 5 miles through the suburbs. Plenty of low gear work.

2 First stretch of dual carriageway. Get up speed over the 23 miles. By-pass Coventry.

3 8 miles down the M45. Only 8 minutes to cover this ground.

4 Really open out now. 59 miles down the M1, at 75-80 mph.

5 Leave the M1 at Watford. Going into North London suburbs on the A41. Average about 30 mph for 10 miles on de-restricted road.

6 Heavy traffic now from Mill Hill, through Hendon, Kilburn, Westminster. 47 minutes for 8 miles. Constant stop-start driving through the motorists' jungle.

7 Victoria Coach Station. Turn-around point. 114 miles from Birmingham. Only 2 hours 55 minutes by Midland Red.

Midland Red coaches provide a high-speed link between London and Birmingham, 364 days a year. To date, they have clocked up over 6,000,000 successful miles. And each motorway coach engine completes a tough 80,000 miles before it is taken out to start a gruelling new life in urban passenger service.

Shell play an important part in this operation. Rotella T in the sump ensures first-class performance all the year round.

GO WELL—GO SHELL

Above: The supercharged Midland Red coach cruises at 80 mph. Shell Rotella T protects its engine against the stresses of continuous motorway running.

BUS & COACH. April 1965

At a time when most coaches still had curved waistrails, a legacy of the pre-war streamline era, the straight-waisted C5s with their distinctive lantern windscreens looked stunning in real life and on posters. As they got older, most were relegated to bus services but did not look out of place.

Far right Among the Day Trips offered was Windsor, including "a drive to the wonderful London Airport" for sightseeing!

Right The rears of the earliest C5s also had the winged logo but most were turned out with this simplified style. This is CM5T 4801 with toilet in the nearside rear. *BMMO*

MIDLAND RED

DAY and HALF-DAY
TOURS and RACE TRIPS
From
BIRMINGHAM
(White Horse Hotel, Gt. Charles St., near Hall of Memory)

BEARWOOD - HARBORNE - QUINTON
WARLEY - SUTTON - KINGSTANDING
ERDINGTON - SOLIHULL - OLTON
ACOCKS GREEN, Etc.

PERIOD

15th Sept. to 21st Sept., 1962

SEATS MAY BE BOOKED AT ANY "MIDLAND RED" OFFICE OR AGENCY

No Telephone Bookings will be accepted

The Friendly "Midland Red"

Interior views of CM5T 4801. The seat moquette was considered very striking at the time. *BMMO*

NON-STOP **MIDLAND RED** NON-STOP

MOTORWAY EXPRESS

Commencing on Monday, November 2nd, 1959

THE FIRST MOTORWAY EXPRESS IN GREAT BRITAIN

THE FIRST MOTORWAY EXPRESS IN GREAT BRITAIN

BIRMINGHAM to LONDON
DAILY

		a.m.*	p.m.	p.m.
BIRMINGHAM (DIGBETH COACH STATION)	depart	8.30*	2.00	6.30
LONDON (VICTORIA COACH STATION)	arrive	11.55	5.25	9.55

LONDON to BIRMINGHAM
DAILY

		a.m.*	p.m.	p.m.
LONDON (VICTORIA COACH STATION)	depart	9.30*	1.30	6.30
BIRMINGHAM (DIGBETH COACH STATION)	arrive	12.55	4.55	9.55

FARES   13/3 single   21/3 return

ALWAYS IN THE LEAD

The Friendly Midland Red

* Due to the ceremony of the opening of the new Motorway, this journey will not be operated on Monday, November 2nd

Printed by Green & Walburn Ltd., B'ham 7.

A second motorway express was soon introduced between London and Coventry, not long afterwards being extended to Nuneaton whose garage provided the coaches. The side destination board of 4800, loading at Pool Meadow, Coventry, has been extended to carry the Nuneaton signwriting. *Maurice Collignon*

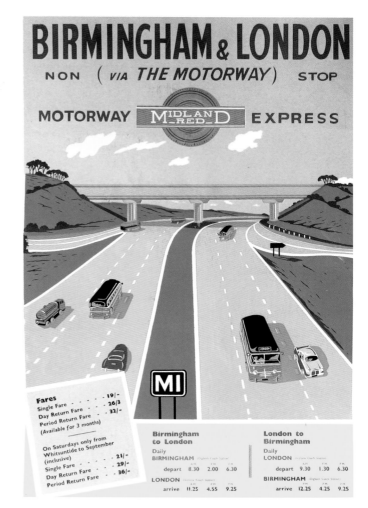

BIRMINGHAM & LONDON
NON (*VIA* THE MOTORWAY) STOP
MOTORWAY **MIDLAND RED** EXPRESS

MI

Fares

Single Fare	- - - -	19/-
Day Return Fare	- - -	26/3
Period Return Fare	-	32/-
(Available for 3 months)		

On Saturdays only from Whitsuntide to September (inclusive)

Single Fare	- - - -	21/-
Day Return Fare	- - -	29/-
Period Return Fare	-	36/-

Birmingham to London
Daily
BIRMINGHAM (Digbeth Coach Station)

depart	8.30	2.00	6.30

LONDON (Victoria Coach Station)

arrive	11.25	4.55	9.25

London to Birmingham
Daily
LONDON (Victoria Coach Station)

depart	9.30	1.30	6.30

BIRMINGHAM (Digbeth Coach Station)

arrive	12.25	4.25	9.25

From a Dream towards a Nightmare

The chassisless D9 was another revolutionary design, described in one trade press review as 'the bus driver's dream of home'. The prototype, 4773, entered service in 1958 with 344 production examples following between 1960 and 1966. 4773 carried a number of front grille designs in its lifetime, this square style being arguably the least attractive. The location is Moat Row, Birmingham, on 4 April 1965. The D9 was indeed a dream to drive but, unfortunately, the company's fortunes meant the world the D9s inhabited was about to turn into a nightmare. Rising costs, fare increases and falling demand were mixed with unreliability caused by traffic congestion and staff shortages into a toxic cocktail that eventually killed the company. *Maurice Collignon*

The D9 was widely considered to be a most handsome bus, despite the change of glazing style in the front and rear domes. They sounded powerful yet the noise was soft and not intrusive. Drivers would confirm that the new 10.5 litre engines really were powerful while the semi-automatic gearbox relieved the weariness of the previous constant-mesh units. Dudley's bus station was located on a steep hill, with the castle as the backdrop, and for many services a challenging place for laden buses to start away from. The 87 terminated at Dudley; in 1970 5326 has set down its remaining passengers at the alighting stop in Birmingham Street and is now turning right for the boarding stop in Fisher Street, thankfully on the flat! The bus station has since been rebuilt so all services can load on the level. *Ken Jubb*

Many D9s were fitted when new with side illuminated advertisements including 4963 on the 130 to Stourbridge, at its terminus in Navigation Street, Birmingham, prior to the opening of the Bull Ring Bus Station. *Alan D Broughall*

Forthcoming Events leaflets were produced regularly throughout the year. The double-deck bus is the new D9 but the drawing is crude compared to earlier efforts.

The two underfloor-engine BMMO D10s were the pinnacle of Midland Red's technical expertise and received an ecstatic response in the trade press when new in 1960-1. It was the D10 that excited the Motor Transport reporter to describe Midland Red as the 'bus operating company which has so often pointed the way for the makers' designers to follow'. In this case the manufacturers did not follow and neither did Midland Red. The D10 was not unsuccessful but its advantage for one-man operation over the simpler D9 was not foreseen at the time. After trials around the network, Stafford became the home of the pair, the first D10, 4943, is seen here departing Cannock for the county town. Happily this stunning example of BMMO technology survives in running condition at The Transport Museum, Wythall. *Ken Jubb*

Left The proportions of 4943's staircase, provided generously with poster cases, impressed the trade press *BMMO. Right* Lower saloon interior of the first D10, 4943, showing the excellent headroom along the gangway, despite the underfloor engine. To avoid raising the floor level, BMMO placed the engine the opposite way round to single-deckers, i.e. with cylinder heads towards the centre and the crankcase towards the nearside. The deepest part of the engine, the flywheel housing, was thus outside the area restricted by legal minimum ground clearance regulations and clear of the lower saloon gangway. *BMMO*

The second D10, 4944, unsuccessfully tested a two-door, twin staircase arrangement, seating only 65, and was rebuilt to single door and staircase in November 1962. *BMMO*

Upper saloon of the two-door D10, clearly showing the front staircase while the mirror at the back corner is a reminder of the exit staircase. The style of fibreglass ceiling with raised sections covering the roof structure will also remind many readers of journeys on D9s. *BMMO*

By 1959 the Cruise fleet was in need of updating and three C2s were modernised with a simpler grille and bumpers comparable to the C4 – one more was treated in 1960. This caused some confusion in the Publicity Department which produced for the 1960 Cruise brochure a picture of a C3 doctored with C2 windscreens, destinations blinds and registration, and a C2 with a C4 grille, windscreens and destination, roof windows, and the registration and unique fleetname of the prototype C4.

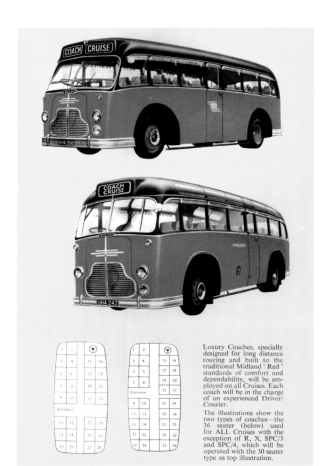

Luxury Coaches, specially designed for long distance touring and built to the traditional Midland 'Red' standards of comfort and dependability, will be employed on all Cruises. Each coach will be in the charge of an experienced Driver/Courier.

The illustrations show the two types of coaches—the 36 seater (below) used for ALL Cruises with the exception of R, X, SPC/3 and SPC/4, which will be operated with the 30 seater type as top illustration.

MidlandRed

The tour coach fleet was relatively small so, rather than design a new fleet for 1962, Midland Red engaged Plaxton to rebody some existing coaches. The bulk were C3s which, in their new lengthened form with Plaxton 'Panorama' bodies, became class CL3 (although initially described as C3L). Three C2s were also rebodied with Plaxton 'Embassy' bodies for tours over narrow roads, to become class CL2 (originally C2L). This gave rise to further adjusted pictures as the 1962 brochure included an insert displaying the new coaches for the season (right). This used Plaxton photographs doctored for the purpose, the C3L having a different window spacing from the actual CL3, whilst the C2L looked particularly wrong being based on the body for the Bedford SB and Ford Thames. The advertised coaches also boasted destination boxes, strangely not fitted to the rebodied vehicles although some later gained them.

The real horror was still to come as they were supplied in an off-white livery. CL3 4220 is seen in Scotland, wearing the off-white (below). *R Mallabon/ The Transport Museum, Wythall*

New Coaches for the 1962 Season

Type C3L (36 seater)

Type C2L (26 seater)

Here are our new 1962 coaches – an entirely new fleet specially designed and built for coach cruising. Special emphasis has been given to more spacious seating and viewing so that 1962 coach cruise travel will provide luxurious comfort and pleasure.

Type C3L will be operating on all cruises with the exception of V, X, SPC/3 and SPC/4. The C2L type will be used for these latter cruises.

Seating Plan overleaf.

1965 coach Cruises
Departing from the Midlands

DEVON · CORNWALL · WALES · SCOTTISH HIGHLANDS

To

All inclusive FARES

MIDLAND RED D

S.W. COAST · IRELAND · SNOWDONIA

SHETLAND ISLES

		£ s d
5 days	DEVON	19 0 0
7 days	WEST COUNTRY	23 10 0
8 days	DEVON & CORNISH RIVIERA	30 0 0
10 days	DEVON & CORNWALL	36 0 0
2 days	SNOWDONIA	6 0 0
5 days	WALES	19 3 0
7 days	OBAN & WESTER HIGHLANDS	28 0 0
7 days	BANCHORY & ABERDEENSHIRE	26 10 0
7 days	GALLOWAY & ISLE OF ARRAN	27 0 0
7 days	GLENCOE & THE WESTERN HIGHLANDS	26 10 0
7 days	ABERDEEN & ROYAL DEESIDE	27 0 0
8 days	WESTERN HIGHLANDS & ARGYLL	30 0 0
8 days	ULLAPOOL & THE NORTH WEST HIGHLANDS	30 0 0
9 days	WESTERN HIGHLANDS & ISLE OF SKYE	35 0 0
9 days	WESTERN HIGHLANDS & ROYAL DEESIDE	34 10 0
11 days	LOCH NESS & THE NORTH WEST	40 0 0
13 days	JOHN O GROATS & WESTER ROSS	48 10 0
*14 days	SHETLAND ISLES	92 0 0
14 days	IRELAND	56 0 0

* No Single Rooms Available

FERBER

BOOK HERE

The off-white was replaced by the proper colours after only one season. Rather longer lasting was the handwritten style of fleetname. This 1965 image shows CL2 3350 after repaint, retaining just a narrow cream band containing the fleetname. *Ken Jubb*

The 1957 series of 50 S15 40-seat dual-purpose buses had black down to the waistrails. The second batch of S15s, a total of 48 built in 1962, had the black restricted to the roofs only, in the style of the C5 family. 5052 loads in Evesham with a Stratford Blue Willowbrook-bodied Leyland PD3 alongside. Separate timetable cases for both operators can be seen. *Barry Le Jeune*

As BMMO production started to decline, orders were placed for Leyland Leopard single-deck buses (and later coaches) and Daimler Fleetline double-deckers, the first being delivered in 1962-3. Twenty of the first hundred Leopards, the LS18 class all built to the new maximum permitted length of 36 feet, were finished as dual-purpose vehicles (LS18A) in red and black livery. These had standard fleetnames instead of the discreet S15 monograms which arguably would have looked lost on these substantially longer vehicles. Strangely, while none of the post-war company-built single-deckers had BMMO badges, these Leylands did. 5194 provides comfortable accommodation on service 709 from Burton's Wetmore Park bus station. *Ken Jubb*

100 BMMO single-deckers were planned for 1962-3, fifty S14 service buses and 50 S15 dual purpose vehicles. In the event only 48 S15s (5045-92) were constructed while the service buses (5095-144) became the 52-seat S16 class, the first vehicles to the 36 feet length and 8 ft 2½ ins width. Rather obviously stretched versions of the S14/S15 with too many side windows, their performance was lacklustre, retaining the 8-litre engine and constant-mesh gearbox. The S17 quickly followed and was much more popular with drivers enjoying the BMMO 10.5 litre engine and semi-automatic gearbox. The first of the 'missing' two vehicles, 5093, became the solitary S19 that was basically the S17 with a modified front axle. 5094 was completed as a further S16, being constructed after 5095-144. *Alan Osborne*

Three S17s, 5722-4, with 1965 registration numbers but not entering service until January 1966, were built as dual-purpose, 48-seat vehicles and designated S21A. Each had different trim and upholstery to gain passenger reaction for future production. They were re-classified S22 in 1967 and S17 upon downgrading to bus status in 1971. *Ken Jubb*

Daimler was particularly pleased that Midland Red had chosen the Fleetline, providing another victory over its longer established rear engine rival, the Leyland Atlantean. 50 were delivered as the DD11 class in 1963, alongside D9s being built by BMMO, and Fleetlines then became the standard double-decker from 1966 to 1970, all with Alexander bodies. Interestingly Midland Red had around 300-350 vehicles in each generation of its double-deckers: this applying to the FEDDs, the early post-war 'worried-look' double-deckers on AEC Regent II (AD2 class) and BMMO D5 chassis, the D7s, the D9s and finally the Fleetlines. 5249 departs Coventry in 1964 on the frequent 658 service to Leicester via Nuneaton and Hinckley. The DD11 Fleetlines boasted illuminated advertisement panels on both sides and, like the Leopards, had BMMO badges. Alexander was well known for its curved screens so it is an interesting demonstration of Midland Red style that the company preferred flat glazing. Sadly, the brightwork provided around the lower screens on the DD11s and DD12s had to be replaced by thick rubber on most examples. *Barry Le Jeune*

149 Fleetlines built between 1966-8 formed the DD12 class. 1966 Fleetline 5993 is at Leamington station, bound for Gaydon on a special RAF display day. The DD12s introduced this rather plain style of MIDLAND fleetname that was also used on C5A vehicles (various types of C5 family downgraded to bus work). Tiny one-inch high fleet numbers briefly became the standard size for newer buses (D9s onwards) from February 1966, as seen here just above the front wheel. Two-inch numbers replaced these almost useless one-inch ones on new deliveries and repaints of newer vehicles from April 1967. Older vehicles continued to have the long-established bigger fleet numbers – this time the D9s were regarded as part of the old school and did not get the two-inch numbers. *Ken Jubb*

The highly successful motorway services warranted coaches to the new permitted length to gain more seats. A prototype 36 feet long coach, no. 5295, entered service in March 1963, designated the CM6T type. This incorporated the 10.5 litre engine with a manual five-speed gearbox, changed after about three months in service to two-pedal semi-automatic. It looked very much like a stretched CM5T, even having the familiar lantern-style windscreens when new. The 29 production BMMO CM6 family of coaches constructed in 1965-6 featured new windscreens and wider pillar spacings – the first such change since 1946! Those with toilets seated 44 compared to only 34 on their CM5T predecessors. A silver version of the handwritten style fleetname was applied to them and the LC7, LC8 and LC9 classes of Leyland Leopard coaches delivered around the same time. Tiny fleet numbers were also employed. The archaic wooden side destination boards on the earlier motorway coaches gave way to illuminated panels. 5661, seen here at Pool Meadow, Coventry, in 1967 carries anti-nationalisation lettering above the panels – a fruitless campaign as Midland Red's owners, British Electric Traction, soon sold out voluntarily to the state. *Ken Jubb*

50 Leyland Leopard coaches were received in 1965, marking a major modernisation of the coach fleet, then still containing many C1s dating back to 1949. 49 were 36 feet long and formed the LC7 class with Duple 49-seat bodies. The forced air ventilation supplemented by opening roof vents often proved inadequate when the coach was parked so it is perhaps not surprising some of the passengers look dozy! *John May*

By 1966, many UK cruises were in the hands of Leyland/Plaxton coaches; 15 new LC9 touring coaches joining the solitary LC8, 5823 new in 1965, which was used in publicity for the 1966 season. *Ken Jubb*

One of the 1966 LC9 coaches, 5826, seen on the Royal Deeside and Wester Ross tour in the company of a David MacBrayne bus. *Ken Jubb*

The handwritten style fleetname style also appeared on some bus leaflets. The company was developing limited stop services in a big way as car travel, encouraged by motorway development around Birmingham, became a chronic threat.

The general appearance of the fleet was declining. In March 1967 repaints had all their brightwork painted red, except ventilators. This saved time masking brightwork but looked terrible and the practice was discontinued in April after four weeks. Vehicles that had suffered in this way remained blighted, one would seem to have been D9 4935, seen with Midland Red tour advertising at Banbury in 1969 after receiving a further repaint. New designs introduced from 1967 lacked rear route number blinds. The blinds were removed from existing vehicles and the glass painted red from January 1970. The first Fleetlines converted to driver only operation had signs that could be switched on, advising pay on entry, fitted in the former illuminated MIDLAND box above the destinations, no doubt taking advantage of the wiring. To avoid potential confusion, the MIDLAND box was painted over on all vehicles as seen here on 4935. The pay on entry signs on Fleetlines were eventually fitted under the top edge of the recessed nearside windscreen, handily adjacent to the entrance door. *Ken Jubb*

BMMO production may have been dropping in the 1960s but equipment suppliers were still proud to be connected with a company bearing such a dynamic reputation. These advertisements include one for the sweaty seats of the latest S21 semi-coaches.

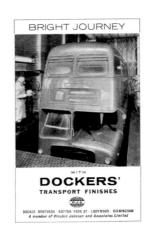

The next BMMO-built buses to follow the S17s were more 36-footers, mechanically almost identical. The body structure, however, was based on the CM6 production coaches, with wider pillar spacings and single rear window with emergency door moved to the offside. Three different interior finishes reflected the work the buses were intended to do. 29 S21 buses with forced ventilation enjoyed semi-coach status and thus a contrasting roof. 5856 has a black roof but maroon was used instead from May 1967 on all coaches and dual-purpose vehicles. It is working the infrequent 545 Market Harborough to Coventry service. *Ken Jubb*

Delivered around the same time were 10 Willowbrook-bodied Leyland Leopards which formed the LS20 class. The LS20 and S21 vehicles brought two-inch fleet numbers and silver fleetnames to dual-purpose buses from 1967. LS20 vehicles were the only post-war buses to lack via blinds until the NBC arrangements imposed by the Leyland Nationals. 5848 is seen at Stratford-upon-Avon where, at this time, vehicles on the long X91 Leicester – Hereford service crossed. The vehicles continued through but the drivers were exchanged at Stratford and returned to their original start point without having to go all the way. *Ken Jubb*

Updating The Image

In addition to the chaos of different fleetnames carried by the vehicles, a neat new style began to appear on publicity from 1967. An early application is seen on the Forthcoming Events leaflet, followed by the finalised style with underlining. These included brochures that now prominently included Continental holidays.

Continental tours were introduced in 1966 in association with a Belgian coach operator. Patrons would fly from Birmingham, and the brochure showed a Van Hool bodied coach with air-conditioning, reclining seats, toilet and Midland Red fleetnames. Tours were offered to Austria, Switzerland, the Venetian Riviera and Ostend.

Continental Cruises justified a separate brochure in 1967, with 15 tours offered across Europe as far as Yugoslavia. The cover showed a charming picture of smartly-dressed holidaymakers in an aeroplane, a small boy in shorts, shirt and tie playing happily on the gangway floor. The tours continued to develop into the 1970s until amalgamation into the National Holidays programme.

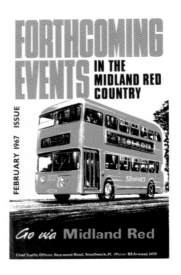

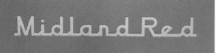

Midland Red

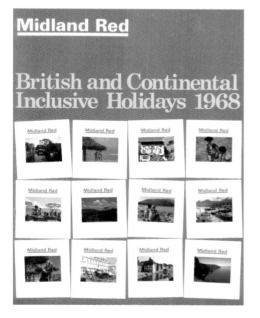

British and Continental Inclusive Holidays 1968

The seating quality was becoming as confusing as the fleetnames with the 29 S21 semi-coaches being followed by the 37 S22 dual-purpose vehicles. Compared to the S21s, the S22s were almost bland with a quieter style of grille and, unfortunately, all-over red livery. They also had a gold version of the handwritten style fleetnames. The S22s had forced ventilation with fixed windows too but 5903, seen here at Bearwood Bus Station, was the exception, having a small number of opening vents. *Ken Jubb*

Midland Red

Carefree by coach-relax in coach comfort

Our Programme provides a large choice of Day and Half-day Excursions from which you can select to spend a day visiting Beauty Spots, Seaside Resorts, Stately Homes, Historic Places, and a host of other interesting places.

Day, Half-day and Evening EXCURSIONS

Programmes giving full details available on request from:

MIDLAND RED ENQUIRY OFFICES

and Agents throughout the Midlands
or direct from

BIRMINGHAM & MIDLAND MOTOR OMNIBUS CO. LTD.

Bearwood Road, Smethwick, Warley, Worcs.

Telephone: 021-429 3030

Maroon began to replace the smart black roof on coaches and dual-purpose vehicles from May 1967, initially with the existing fleetname styles. On some classes the maroon was extended down to waist level which was perhaps not an improvement. LC7 class 1965 Duple-bodied Leyland Leopard 5799 at Cardiff bus station. *Ken Jubb*

The motorway days of former CM5T 4811 should have been long gone but, at Worcester in 1969, a duty calls on one of the expresses up the M5 to Birmingham. *Ken Jubb*

The style of fleetname used for a while on publicity was extended to the vehicles themselves from the end of 1968 and started to bring an end to a very confused period. There was a silver version for coaches and dual-purpose vehicles and gold for service buses. 103 DD13 dual-door buses intended from new as driver only vehicles would prove to be virtually the last double-deckers purchased new by the company – only two more came in 1974, the result of an order placed by Harper Brothers, taken over by Midland Red, and carrying ECW bodies. The DD13's centre-exit doors were notoriously little used by Midland Red drivers! New 6197, exiting Pool Meadow bus station, Coventry, in 1969 shows the gold version of the new fleetname and also the cast aluminium version in similar style on the front dash panel, replacing the BMMO badge used on earlier vehicles. *Ken Jubb*

Other carriers of the gold version included the five 1960 Weymann Fanfare-bodied Leyland Leopards bought in 1970 and originally in the Sheffield Joint Omnibus Committee fleet. Despite the coach bodies, the gold fleetname meant they were clearly intended for more mundane duties. 6260 (6174 WJ) is seen at Central Works after preparation for its new career with Midland Red. The age discrimination on vehicles receiving the new fleetnames and two-inch fleet numbers remained until June 1970, from when they were applied to all repaints, including a few D7s. *Ken Jubb*

5295 (5495 HA) was the prototype CM6T, new in 1963 and is seen at Central Works in 1970. As a coach, it had received the silver version of the fleetname but, as can be seen, this sat among earlier styles with the handwritten style name in cast metal on the front and the anachronistic side boards lettered in gold. *Ken Jubb*

Midland Red in 1969 took delivery of a batch of Leyland Leopards with Plaxton's new Elite coach body. There was considerable surprise, therefore, when the 30 LC11 service coaches delivered in 1970 bore the earlier Panorama style although with much tidier side trim. Some were delivered with single windscreens due to supplier shortages, Midland Red's preferred divided screens being soon substituted. Leopard/ Plaxton Panorama 6251 leaves Chatsworth House in Derbyshire on 18 April 1971. *E V Trigg*

After years of simplifying the livery it was a bit of a surprise to find the cheap-and-cheerful Ford/ Plaxton Derwents received from 1970 had the luxury of cream relief bands! Numerically the first, 6294, looks immaculate at Central Works before entering service. *Ken Jubb*

Left Stand 16 in Shrewsbury's main bus station in summer 1971 boasted an interesting pair of stop plates attached to the traditional wheel symbol and destination summary. There is a very tasty Associated Motorways plate for the long-distance coach network as well as a rather home-made approximation of the new fleetname on the company's own stop for tours and excursions, both about to be overwhelmed by NATIONAL white branding.
Right The departure stand information board at Worcester's Newport Street bus station in early 1971 shows only a small trace of the devastation to services to come. A fibreglass timetable case with the latest fleetname style is alongside. *Ken Jubb*

Stratford Blue

The Stratford Blue subsidiary, to all intents, appeared completely independent of Midland Red. Although livery and lettering was simplified and modernised over the years, the Stratford Blue fleet continued to present a traditional air. Dependant in its earlier years on second-hand Tilling-Stevens buses, post-World War Two modernisation brought a fine fleet of Leylands, almost inevitably clad in Flowers brewery advertisements. The double-deckers were Leyland-bodied PD2 Titans of which no 39 (GUE 245) dated from 1948. Alongside in this September 1962 view of the Red Lion bus station, Stratford, is 18 (2768 NX), one of a trio of 1960 Leyland PD3s with Willowbrook bodies representing a new generation. Parent company Midland Red, with plenty of experience of the front entrance configuration, continued to favour rear entrances for its front-engined buses. *Roy Marshall*

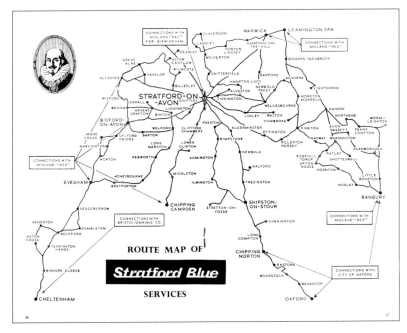

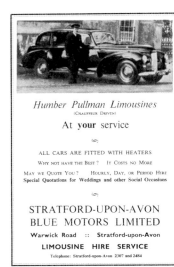

An unusual activity for a BET subsidiary was Bridgetown Filling Station, owned by Stratford Blue since its earliest days as a private company. The service station was near the centre of Stratford, just across Clopton Bridge at the junction of the roads to Banbury and Oxford, and was sold in 1970. Stratford Blue also ran two chauffeur-driven Humber Pullman limousines from 1951 to 1962.

Leyland PD3s delivered at the very end of 1963 carried a new style of fleetname. Among the first of the older buses to be repainted with the new style was no 21 (TNX 455), a 1956 Leyland PD2/12 bodied by Willowbrook, a regular supplier to Stratford Blue from 1950 onwards. It is seen at the exit to the garage at Stratford under some impressive signwriting. *R Mallabon/ The Transport Museum, Wythall*

Timetable

with services of all operators in
South Warwickshire

commencing

21st May, 1966

1/-

until
5th May, 1967
or until further notice

A livery simplification was to delete the silver roofs as double-deck buses were repainted. For a tiny operation, Stratford Blue seemed numerically illiterate, having a lot of trouble with fleet and service numbers. JUE 353 was a Leyland Tiger PS2 single-deck rebuild, receiving in 1961 this graceless 63-seat body by Roe, incorporating Park Royal parts intended for AEC Bridgemasters. In its rebodied form it was numbered 16, continuing the march backwards from no 39 begun in 1948 for double-deck buses. After a second generation 32-9 arrived in 1963, no 16 was renumbered 31 two years later. Although the fleet only numbered 30-40 vehicles, Stratford Blue boasted two garages. The principal one was in Stratford but this is the smaller one at Kineton, opened in 1954 to replace earlier premises alongside taken over from the Kineton Green bus company. *Ken Jubb*

End Game

Midland Red's new fleetnames lacked impact on the vehicles themselves so beefed-up versions, outlined in black, were introduced from October (gold) and November (silver) 1970. On the debit side, even coaches became painted red all over. Among early repaints with the new style was newly absorbed ex-Stratford Blue 1959 Leyland Tiger Cub/ Willowbrook 2041, combining the improved fleetname with the then current style of fleet number, seen above the front side window. A thicker version of the two-inch fleet numbers to match the improved fleetnames followed in early 1971. Legal addresses in matching style were also adopted although arguably this was less successful, being somewhat intrusive. Fleet numbers on the front were standard Stratford Blue practice and the new thicker digits were added to the front of 2041 as seen here. This practice was extended to the entire Midland Red fleet on repaints from this time. 2041 did not last long with Midland Red as all the Leyland Tiger Cubs were withdrawn in April and May 1971. *Ken Jubb*

Stratford Blue's coach fleet were among those receiving the improved silver fleetname upon repaint. Here 1964 thirty feet long Leyland Leopard L2T/ Plaxton 'Panorama' 41-seater 2056 (AAC 21B) tackles the big city. *Alan Osborne*

Midland Red continued to purchase very appealing dual-purpose Leyland Leopards throughout the 1970s, well into the NBC era and minimising the number of Leyland Nationals received. This is one of the 1971 batch that had Willowbrook 49-seat bodies, classified S24 – the letter prefix for non-BMMO types having been abandoned. Fallen leaves eddy around 6416 in Hagley Road West, Birmingham, on 16 November 1971, before that road was converted to a dual carriageway. The run to Ludlow is a delight, see next page. *E V Trigg*

The gold fleetname on Midland Red's first Leyland National. Fleet numbers reached 6473 and then reverted to 101 with this National which marked the end of Midland Red style as 102 upwards were supplied in National Bus Company corporate liveries. *Ken Jubb*

After the 1970 LC11 Plaxton Panorama coaches, Midland Red conformed by purchasing Plaxton's Elite style. Some were on the shorter Leyland PSU4 Leopard chassis for tours, with an overall length of 31 feet. This included the 1971-2 C12 class, the first of which was 6446, seen at Oxford on 23 July 1972. These seated 40; earlier short Leopards only seated 36. *Maurice Collignon*

Some of the final leaflets issued before the National corporate style took over. The London service was now named the *Expressway* with updated CM6T coaches. The 1972 brochure would have been developed the previous year just as National Bus Company management imposed white 'National' coach livery on all its subsidiaries. This carried a heavy price for operators like Midland Red as the extensive goodwill built up by the company was swept aside. Tours and excursions clients who traditionally travelled by Midland Red were particularly deterred by the sight of white express coaches rendered grubby after the slightest shower.

After the split of the old company in 1981, the new Midland Red North company endeavoured to benefit from traditional Midland Red style. For a time the company's buses carried the MIDLAND fleetname and were repainted red all over but the shade was much too dark and quickly looked drab. An earlier attempt to capture the style was the use of semi-preserved D9 5399. Among its duties were three summer Sunday round journeys on the Birmingham to Ludlow service, publicised as the Severn Valley Special. The service from Birmingham via Kidderminster and Bewdley to Ludlow was introduced in stages, with buses finally running through from 1932. The second issue of the Midland Red Bulletin in October 1932 listed the Clee Hills, at 1254 ft, as the highest point served by Midland Red service routes. The road between Ludlow and Cleobury Mortimer is still difficult. The Angel Bank incline from Ludlow onto the Clee Hills is punishing whether ascending or descending while the road descends and winds dangerously through Hopton Wafers. 5399 is seen on Sunday 25 July 1982 on its first journey from Ludlow to Birmingham. It has descended from the Clee Hills in the background, and is now climbing up from Hopton Wafers towards Cleobury Mortimer. *Roger Torode*

Staff Bulletins

The Midland Red Bulletin was first issued in September 1932, edited by James Savage. OCP had initially resisted calls for such a periodical, as he had experience of similar publications fading after the initial enthusiasm. But he agreed that it should be published "to try and weld together the different groups of men who are working with one common aim all over the system, *viz*: To keep the Midland "Red" flag flying at the top of the mast". He need not have been concerned. The first issue was 4 pages long and was distributed free to traffic staff. Subsequent issues cost 1d and the Bulletin quickly increased to 12 pages. It gained a coloured cover from 1934, conducted a tour of the garages and their staff, included news and articles on senior personnel and long-serving staff of 'the old brigade' who had started with horse buses or trams. A network of correspondents in the garages supplied news of sports and social events.

The Bulletin grew to a large magazine of 40 pages with commercial advertising, descriptions of Midland towns and beauty spots, short stories and articles of general interest. Sold by conductors on their buses, sales regularly exceeded 10,000 a month. From March 1937 it became the 'Midland "Red" *Traffic Department* Magazine'. Issue no 85 of September 1939 celebrated the Magazine's birthday and looked forward to further improvements, but with the outbreak of war, this was the last issue.

The original Midland "Red" Bulletin was printed in black and white with this masthead. The January 1933 issue had cheery New Year greetings featuring 1929 MM HA5008.

The Bulletin was renamed in 1937 and contained a range of articles of transport, Midlands and general interest, together with short stories.

A colour cover was introduced in 1934. By now, the Bulletin was intended for passengers and staff.

CONDUCTOR JIM DUTTON

Conductor Jim Dutton of Stourbridge was applauded in the February 1935 Midland "Red" Bulletin for selling over 1,000 copies a month on his bus. Clearly a modest man, he wrote to the Bulletin to explain his success, saying that "I only put it down to PERSEVERANCE, PERSONALITY and POPULARITY." He achieved 1,000 a month on two occasions, and 890 in seven days for the Christmas Number, and he challenged other conductors to beat his record.

Two years later "Fatty" Dutton was again applauded for selling an average of 750 copies of each issue, and working steadily towards his ambition of 50,000 copies overall. Staff at Swadlincote, Kidderminster and Wolverhampton also received praise for their efforts.

The Bulletin resumed in 1946, edited by W H Pine and distributed free 'for staff information only – not for publication'. As in 1932, this commenced with four pages but soon grew, generally having 16 pages. Mr Sinclair saw it as a means of communicating with his staff throughout the company. The garage sports and social activities were accompanied by his encouragement to perform better and dress smarter, together with developments in the company and bus industry, educational items on engineering matters and road traffic law. There were regular jokes, cartoons and anecdotes from the garages. When there were strikes, Mr Sinclair made his feelings clear. The back cover always quoted 'Pats on the Back' for staff from public letters, but there was also the occasional 'Kicks in the Pants' column.

W H Pine edited the Bulletin until his retirement in 1968. It became bi-monthly in 1969 and in 1970 was contracted out to a publisher. It closed in December 1972 after issue 287, to be replaced by an NBC newspaper.

The Staff Information Bulletin from 1946 had a plain design and reflected the gradual build-up of the Company's operations after the war. From 1948, an attractive masthead featuring the S6 was introduced (above).

From December 1950 (top left) the cover featured a bus stop design set into the landscape. The December 1951 issue included Christmas greetings featuring a C1 coach on tour.

The Coronation issue of May 1953 introduced stylised drawings of an S13, LD8 and C2. The following April (top centre) the cover showed two buses pausing in Groby, Leicestershire, for the Quorn hounds to pass with their huntsman. A Triumph Roadster and an Austin Three-way van lead the queue of vehicles.

Drawings of the D7, S14 and C3 appeared from October 1955, and these were regularly updated from then on. This June 1956 issue (bottom left) had one of Mr Sinclair's regular exhortations to his staff to try harder.

From October 1958, D9 prototype 4773 was shown together with an S14 and C5 (bottom right).

These Bulletins have been copied from bound volumes and in some cases it has not been possible to show the full left hand margin.

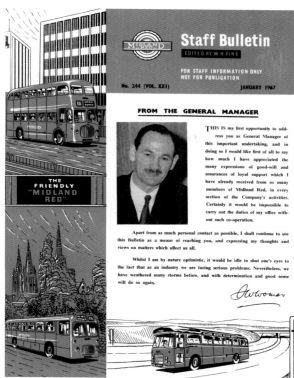

Four examples of the Staff Bulletin from 1962 to 1971.

The April 1962 issue (*top left*) has a production D9 with the S14 and C5. Mr Sinclair uses a Punch cartoon to advise on good customer relations.

In January 1967 (*top right*), JW Womar introduced himself as the new General Manager following Donald Sinclair's retirement. He is accompanied by an updated fleet of D9, S17 and CM6T.

The fleet was further updated in this October 1968 edition (*bottom left*) with DD13, S22 and CM6T vehicles.

Issue 278 from March 1971 (*bottom right*), was produced by professional publishers who still provided a stirring message to the troops.

Properties Style

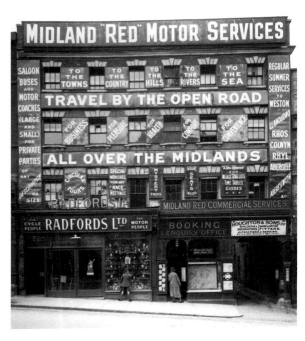

Leamington enquiry office with a fine set of display advertisements. The photographer can be seen reflected in the window. *BMMO, courtesy The Kithead Trust*

Top left Midland Red had an enquiry office in the Bull Ring, its frontage liberally covered in brash red and white enamel signs, also home to the Long-Distance Services department after transfer from Bearwood in 1930. The company had to give up these offices in 1937, moving around the corner to more tastefully decorated premises in Worcester Street, a former gentlemen's clothing emporium. *The Transport Museum, Wythall, archive*

The June 1935 issue of the Midland Red Bulletin included this page of garages decorated for the Silver Jubilee of King George V.

The company had booking offices in many towns, in addition to those with garages. Mr Arthur Guise stands outside the office in Victoria Square, Droitwich, in 1955. The style favoured by Mr Sinclair and his team was much less flamboyant than Mr Power. Both outside and inside are colourful posters of the style illustrated in this book. Mr Guise's sister, Nelly, and Mrs Snow, deal with enquiries. You could get information on any of Midland Red's 1,150 bus services, major or minor, anywhere in the Midlands, from the timetable books held at the enquiry offices and, of course, book on tours and excursions.
BMMO

As the fleet expanded in the early post-war travel boom, garage building and rebuilding continued too. The land for this new garage in Myton Road, Leamington, was acquired in 1936 but, with nothing on the ground by the outbreak of World War Two and post-war building restrictions, the new garage was not opened until 1 September 1957. It replaced elderly premises in Emscote, Warwick. Another garage was located on Old Warwick Road, opposite Leamington station. The colour of brick, used with stone facings, the style of windows, often employing at least one curved corner, and the unusual semi-circular pillars made of bricks laid vertically either side of the bus entrance/exit were features regularly found on the company's early post-war building projects. *Ken Jubb*

Midland Red operated from over thirty garages at the height of passenger demand. Typical of the many new garages built between the two world wars was Redditch, opened in 1931 and seen in 1969. Similar red brick frontages, with regularly spaced recessed rows of bricks and modest ornamentation, could be found all over the system. *Ken Jubb*

This is another typical early post-war Midland Red garage with the wheel symbol above the entrance. These premises were opened in September 1954 in Lichfield, one of the last Midlands centres to receive a garage as decline was about to set in. Outside is bus 4843, one of the two 1949 Guy Arab III vehicles with Barnaby 35-seat bodies, acquired with the business of Kemp & Shaw, Leicester. The restriction caused by the side flashes meant these two Guys had a style of fleetname normally carried by service vehicles. *Ken Jubb*

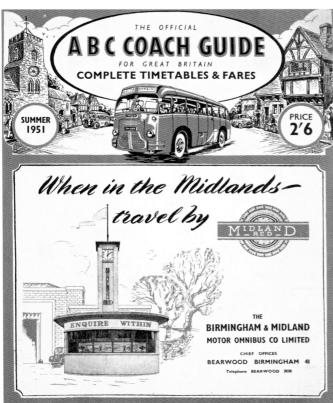

A long-standing painted sign on the wall of the Enquiry Office in Railway Terrace, Rugby. *Patrick Kingston*

Wolverhampton garage notice. Mr Womar's name has replaced that of Mr Sinclair who retired at the end of 1966. *Ken Jubb*

A drawing of a C2, disguised in a non-standard livery, represented the industry on the cover of the Summer 1951 ABC Coach Guide. Also doctored was the illustration of Oldbury garage enquiry office in the Midland Red advert below as ENQUIRE WITHIN was actually MIDLAND RED in real life. Oldbury was in the northern tip of Worcestershire before local government reorganisation in 1974 and known worldwide for its industries, particularly tubes and chemicals. Its Midland Red garage opened on 12 April 1937 and included this Art Deco frontage with round fronted enquiry office and clock tower above. The clock tower was removed in 1968.

Leicester's large garage in Sandacre Street was opened on 1 February 1937, handily adjacent to St Margaret's Bus Station, opened in an incomplete state in July 1942, during the dark days of World War Two. The style of company name above the doorways is typical of its date of construction. Not much sign, however, of BMMO bus production in this view. Bus 4848 (HJU 546) was a 1952 Leyland-bodied Royal Tiger PSU1/9 taken into stock in 1959 with the business of Boyer of Rothley. It is flanked on either side by AD2 class AEC Regents. *Ken Jubb*

Leicester's Southgate Street garage opened on 21 July 1927 with a capacity of 90 vehicles. Architecturally it presented a number of different faces to the world with the entrance/exit to Southgate Street itself being the least flattering. Nevertheless it offers a brave sight after the painters had visited it and applied the latest lettering in 1969. *Ken Jubb*

Such a large company needed a central overhaul works and Midland Red, of course, had gone further and designed and built its own vehicles. It had purchased a site of approximately seven acres off Carlyle Road, Edgbaston, in two parts in 1920 and 1924. Already on the site were buildings used for aircraft construction in World War One. Plans were drawn up during World War Two for everything to be concentrated on the Carlyle site. Engine construction and overhaul would move from Bearwood garage and facilities to construct bodies in quantity would become available. Early post-war building licensing constraints delayed plans but reconstruction work began in 1947. The new complex was launched as 'Central Works' on 25th November 1954 as part of the company's Golden Jubilee celebrations although most continued to call it 'Carlyle'. It bore the same external architectural styling details as the garages constructed around the same time, as can be seen in several pictures in this book. This is the Body Shop around 1954, capable of holding 50 vehicles undergoing overhaul or repair. The two SONs on the left have been through the hot spray paint booth and are awaiting removal of overspray. Traditional livery was still being applied at this time so, in addition to the usual transfers, the SONs would also receive black wings, yellow lining and silver roofs. *BMMO*

Birmingham's gloomy and fume challenged Digbeth coach station opened in 1929 but drew criticism for decades. Vehicles entered at the Rea Street end, 1966 BMMO CM6T 5672 is seen leaving via the exit in Mill Lane during 1970. Subsequent improvements were blighted by proposals to move to other locations but, finally, modern facilities opened at Digbeth in 2010. *David Barber collection*

Timetables

We finish with those unsung volumes that were such a vital part of transporting us from one part of the Midland Red legend to another. A small tribute to the men and women, and their countless hours of effort, arranging those buses to be there to carry us, and carefully transferring those timings into our humble timetable books and leaflets.

Earlier timetables are shown on page 15. From November 1922, timetable covers were in a deep red shade with a line drawing of the latest bus, sometimes surrounded by a stylised radiator (*top row*). By the late 1920s, timetable books were issued twice each year for six districts: Birmingham, Worcester, Shrewsbury, Stafford, Leamington and Leicester. Each was to a page size of 105x165mm. While the 1914 timetable had 24 pages, issued free, the 1932 Birmingham book (*top row, right*) ran to 500 pages, including express services and summaries of holiday tours. Advertising by local businesses was an important feature.

The two full colour covers (*middle row*) were introduced in 1935 and continued in use through the war until replaced in 1947. That with four vehicles was used in all areas but the rather old-fashioned single-decker was used only for Birmingham editions, and it is difficult to determine what type of bus it is supposed to be!

The first timetables after the war continued the pre-war artwork which included the bonneted open charabancs that would not be seen again as the last generation had been rebuilt into forward control service buses.

Mr Sinclair was not the showman Mr Power appears to have been and booking offices, literature etc adopted a much quieter tone. The style of timetable cover (*bottom row, left*) was adopted from March 1947. The page size was increased from 1953 to 134 x 210mm, and the new logo introduced in the late 1960s.